# Southern California
# Luiseño Indian Baskets

# Southern California Luiseño Indian Baskets

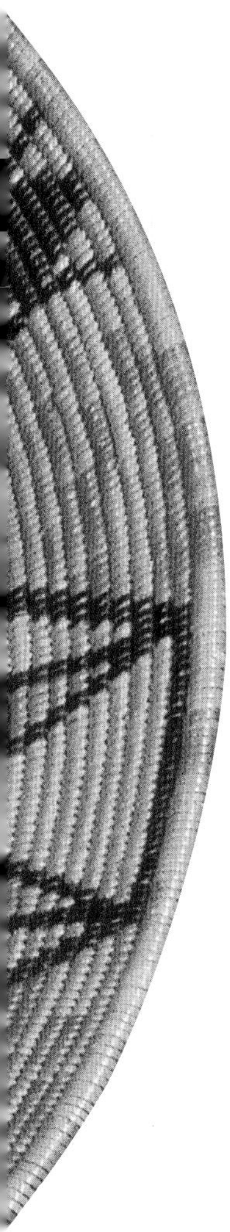

# Southern California Luiseño Indian Baskets

A Study of Seventy-Six Luiseño Baskets
in the Riverside Municipal Museum Collection

by
Justin F. Farmer (Ipai)

with an introduction by
Dr. H. Vincent Moses, Director
Riverside Municipal Museum

First Edition
December 2004

Published by

The Justin Farmer Foundation
A Privately Endowed Charitable Fund
Mr. Joe Moreno, Foundation Chairman
1954 Evergreen Avenue,
Fullerton, California 92835
(714) 256-1260

The book is published on the occasion of the exhibition *Southern California Luiseño Indian Baskets,* and is dedicated to the memory of the late Dr. Christopher Moser, curator of anthropology at the Riverside Municipal Museum from 1979 to 2003. The exhibition has been held at the Riverside Municipal Museum from Fall 2004 through Spring 2005.

ISBN 0-9761492-1-4

Published in the United States by the Justin Farmer Foundation.

Printed in China

Cover image: **Wide La Jolla Tray,** "five petal flower with water bugs"— circa 1890. Collected by Harwood Hall on the La Jolla Reservation. Hall noted that the maker, whom he failed to name, was killed in an earthquake in 1899.

Selected by the US Postal Service to join nine other Indian art pieces for an August 2004 issue of 37 cent postage stamps commemorating the opening of the new NMAI (National Museum of the American Indian) museum in Washington D.C.

Jacket and book design by David Alcorn, Alcorn Publication Design
Printing and binding by C&C Offset Printing Co., Ltd.

# Contents

In August, 2004, the US Postal Service issued a pane of ten 37 cent stamps, commemorating the grand opening of the Smithsonian's new National Museum of the American Indian (NMAI) in Washington, D.C.
The event was also celebrated in Riverside, California, by an exhibition of approximately 76 Luiseño Indian baskets from Riverside and San Diego Counties. The 37 cent stamp in the lower right corner of the pane depicts a magnificent basket from the Riverside Municipal Museum's collection. It was the impetus for this exhibition catalogue.

***Maria Subish holding rattlesnake basket***

This is perhaps one of the most widely circulated photographs depicting a Southern California Indian lady weaving a basket. It was taken by the late Edward Davis of Mesa Grande, San Diego County. This image was reproduced from an original print which was given to the author by Mr. Davis' granddaughter, Mrs. Ann Davis, also of Mesa Grande.

The undated photograph portrays Maria Subish (?Balenzuela) of Mesa Grande, San Diego county. George Wharton suggested that Mrs. Subish (Balenzuela) created this rattlesnake design circa 1899, almost simultaniously with Mrs. Mary Snyder, a Chemhuevi lady, who is generally considered to be the originator of rattlesnake motifs on an Indian basket. The possible conflicting last names reflect notes in Moser's *Native American Basketry of Southern California,* page 130, and notes on the packet enclosing an original print in the author's possession. It is possible that one, or both are married names.

# Introduction

By Dr. H. Vincent Moses

I am proud to introduce this important book about the Riverside Municipal Museum's Luiseño basket collection. Justin Farmer (Ipai) is a recognized authority in the field of Southern California Indian baskets, and we are privileged to have him apply his knowledge and skills in the presentation of the Museum's significant Luiseño basket holdings

The baskets presented on these pages constitute an important part of the Riverside Municipal Museum's founding donations. These objects were chosen from among the collections of three original donors to the Museum; Cornelius Earle Rumsey, Harwood Hall, and Frank Augustus Miller. All three men were adherents of the arts and crafts movement of the early twentieth century and viewed Indian artifacts as American cathedrals of artisanship. Rumsey and Hall featured "Indian" rooms in their homes and Miller displayed Indian artifacts throughout his Mission Inn hotel. They all belonged to the "Mission" Indian Federation of Southern California, where they advocated for improvements in treatment of Native Americans.

The Cornelius Rumsey collection of American Indian materials made the Riverside Municipal Museum possible. Mr. Rumsey retired to Riverside in 1899. During the intervening years, until his death in 1911, he and his wife were active in civic affairs and in acquisition of Native American art pieces. Their personal collection included hundreds of significant Southern California Indian baskets, and other artifacts from Western Indian tribes. In 1924 Mrs. Rumsey gave the Rumsey holdings to the City of Riverside pending creation of a suitable facility to house them. Mayor S.C. Evans Jr. accepted the offer and on December 12, 1925, the Cornelius E. Rumsey Indian Museum opened in the new City Hall basement.

Harwood Hall, during the early twentieth century, served as the US Bureau of Indian Affairs' Superintendent of the Sherman Institute (now Sherman High School), in Riverside. Hall participated in the "Mission" Indian Federation of Southern California, along with other civic leaders. His position with the Sherman Institute and the Federation, presented him opportunities to collect prime items not necessarily available to other collectors. As you will learn from Justin Farmer, Harwood Hall, unlike Cornelius Rumsey, acquired only the best baskets available. The baskets in his collection represent only the most spectacular and pristine baskets available. The basket on the cover of Justin's book is from the Hall collection (#A8-100) and was created on the La Jolla reservation in the 1890's by a lady who was killed in the 1899 Christmas Day earthquake.

Baskets donated by Frank A Miller, builder and master of the Mission Inn hotel in Riverside, constitutes the third principal source of objects for this publication. Miller, like Hall, appears to have sought only the best examples of American Indian art objects, so his baskets cannot be viewed as being typical, in the broadest sense of the word. They are, however, quite indicative of the skills and artistry of Luiseño basket makers.

The spectacular Luiseño basket, featured on the cover of this publication, joined nine other Indian art pieces as images on an USPS postage stamp pane issued in 2004 to commemorate opening of the National Museum of the American Indian in Washington D.C. Inclusion of this Luiseño basket came about thanks to the steadfast work of the late Dr. Christopher Moser, curator of anthropology at the Riverside Municipal Museum from 1979 to 2003. Unfortunately, Dr. Moser died suddenly of cancer in January 2003, before having an opportunity to see the stamp issued to the public.

Over the 23+ years Dr. Moser served as Curator of anthropology, he and Justin worked very closely analyzing and cataloguing the Museum's collection of Indian baskets and researching basket makers. It was the dream of both Dr. Moser and Justin that a detailed catalogue of the Museum's Indian baskets, and their provenance, would someday evolve. Issuance of the 2004 USPS stamp pane offered an impetus for such a catalogue. Although Dr. Moser is no longer with us, I am happy to say that the Museum and readers of this fine work are beneficiaries of Justin's and "Chris's" dream.

Please enjoy your journey into the realm of these marvelous works of art and culture.

Dr. H. Vincent Moses
Museum Director
September, 2004

# Southern California
# Luiseño Indian Baskets

***Esperanza Sobenish (Johanish) weaving a very large basket***

Mr. Edward Davis photographed Esperanza Sobenish on the Rincon reservation in 1919
as she created a very large basket with numerous zoomorphic features, such as rattlesnakes
and birds. This basket, when completed, became a rather wide low basin and is believed to
be in the possession of a collector in San Bernadino county, California. An original photograph, from which this image was taken, is in the author's collection who received
it from Mrs. Ann Davis, Edward Davis' granddaughter.

# CHAPTER 1

# Southern California Indians, Their Genesis, And Their Baskets

Before discussing Luiseño or "Mission Indian" baskets in detail, it might be proper to discuss the general term "Mission", which is very frequently used in connection with baskets from Southern California. To understand this term . . . "Mission". . . it is necessary that the reader have at least a nodding acquaintance with early Spanish history in California, particularly pertaining to its Catholic missions. Although the Spanish Catholic church established and maintained a mission system virtually throughout North and South America during the 17th, 18th, and 19th centuries, the lasting impact on local natives was quite different in California than elsewhere.

**History of Alta California**

With but a few minor exceptions, California was never visited by Europeans prior to the year 1769. Those minor exceptions were exceedingly rare sightings, and even more rare landings of Spaniard, Russian, or English sailing vessels. However, there were no Non-Indians residing permanently in what is now California prior to 1769.

In the summer of 1769, Fr. Junipero Serra, a Spanish Franciscan priest, lead an excursion into, and established a Catholic mission at, what is now San Diego. Within a matter of days after establishing that first mission, which he named *San Diego de Alcala'*, Junipero Serra traveled north to what is known today as Monterey, in central California. Here he established a colony, which was to become the Spanish capitol of *Alta (northern)* California for nearly a century. Indeed, Monterey was also the site of California's first State Capitol in 1850. During the period 1769 to 1824, the Spanish Catholic church established 21 missions, from San Diego, on the south, to Sonoma (north of San Francisco) on the north. Although Mexico gained its independence from Spain circa 1823, Monterey remained capitol of Alta California until 1846, when California, as a result of the "Bear Flag Revolt", became a sovereign republic. Within approximately a week, Alta California was seized by the US military, after which it became a US territorial holding of the United States of America. California formally joined the USA as the 31st state in 1850.

History tells us that the missions were established for the purpose of *"reducing"* the native Indian population to "children" of the Spanish Catholic church. This is, in part, true. However, in order to maintain a church in a region many thousands of miles from the mother country, the missionaries had to support both themselves and their neophyte "children" (converts). This meant forcibly removing Indian families from their traditional villages, housing them in a church owned and operated enclave, and reducing them to herdsmen and dirt farmers. This also meant feeding and clothing them. Each of the 21 missions was operated as an autonomous entity with a cadre of Spaniards, both cleric and military.

In reality, California Catholic missions evolved into huge cattle ranches, some of which ran upwards of, or even in excess of, 50,000 head of cattle, horses and sheep. Sale of hides and tallow (fat for candles and soap) were the basic commodities which financially supported the mission-ranches. Quite obviously, cattle ranches of this magnitude required huge numbers of laborers and support personnel. Also quite obviously, the only source of laborers in the late 1700's was the local Indian population. As might be expected, the Spanish military "recruited" local Indians, both male and female, from local Indian villages and marched them to the missions, where they were introduced to the myriad of duties necessary to the maintenance and operation of these ranch-cities (aka Missions). For sake of expediency, missionary priests paid little or no attention to established tribal boundaries or languages and lumped all Indians together into one work force, regardless of what language was spoken or what their culture might be. For whatever reason, all Indians under control of a given mission were assigned one name reflecting the mission to which they were bound; e.g. all Indians within the lands claimed by the mission at San Diego de Alcala' were assigned the name *San Diegueños*. In later years the *San* was dropped but the name *Diegueño* continues to this day. Likewise, Indians assigned to the Mission at San Luis Rey de Francia were given the name *San Luiseños*. As with the Diegueños, the *San* was later dropped and the people became known as *Luiseños*. Indians at other missions underwent similar generic renaming.

Alta California's mission system blossomed in the late 18th century and the first several decades of the 19th century, during which time literally thousands of local Indians were pressed into *involuntary servitude* to support the Spanish Catholic church, the Spanish crown, and its cattle ranches. Entire native villages were decimated and ceased to function due to forced relocation of their Indian residents . . . men, women, and children. Mission cattle were allowed to forage over lands, and devour plants and seeds, which for tens of centuries supported a large Indian population. Wild game found themselves in competition with imported ranch animals and thus were also decimated. Even had Indians not been forced into servitude at these mission-ranches, they could not have survived competition from the mission's cattle.

In 1823, New Spain (now called Mexico) conducted a successful revolution, established themselves as a sovereign republic, and assumed control over Alta California. All Spanish persons associated with the 21 missions were purged and replaced by those from Mexico. Almost immediately the mission empire, established by the Spanish missionaries, began its collapse. Within approximately 10 years, the entire mission system became defunct and secularized. Church sanctuary buildings returned to the local secular priest but the heart of the cattle ranch simply *came apart at the seams*. The vast cattle herds and land holdings were meted out to prominent Mexican residents via *Mexican Land Grants*. Huge cattle herds were reportedly slaughtered for the pure sport of it, or turned loose to run wild and complete the devastation of Indian lands. Mr. Edward J.F. Mast, of Yolo County traces his heritage back into the middle 1800's and reports that circa 1850 **one** herd of horses was estimated to be 10 miles long in the San Joaquin Valley. It takes a lot of wild grass and seeds to feed that many animals. Those grasses and seeds were a major source of food for the local Indians. Former mission buildings were either abandoned, demolished, or burned and their range animals released to run semi-wild. Indians who had been neophytes for decades, some for an entire life, were turned out to forage for themselves with only the clothes on their back. Even some sanctuary buildings were razed for their construction materials, or used as barns or out-buildings (as was the case of the grand old church at San Luis Rey in the middle-late 1800's, when the author's grandparents were married by the secular priest).

By the late 1830's California was in almost complete collapse. Americans, had gained substantial control over Southern California politics and economy, while in Central and Northern California, the Swiss (General Sutter at Sacramento) and the Russians (Fort Ross) dominated.

In the summer of 1846 several dozen Americans waged a blood-less revolution, called *The Bear Flag Rebellion,* wrested control of Alta California from the then Mexican governor, and declared California to be a sovereign republic (nation). Within a few weeks, the United States assumed authority over the newly created California Republic and in 1850, California became an official state of the Union.

**Southern California Missions**

Although the original Spanish Catholic mission network ceased to function as autonomous cattle ranch/religious missions after the middle 1830's, some retained their congregation, and in a few cases even used their original parish buildings well into the 20th century. Indeed, a few of the original buildings, albeit renovated, are still in use as parish churches. Most are *places of historical interest* which maintain their original name, and the Indians living within the church hinterlands are still referred to by a mission-related name; e.g.

| Original Mission Name | Present Indian Name |
|---|---|
| Mission San Diego de Alcala' (1769) | Diegueño |
| Mission San Luis Rey de Francia (1798) | Luiseño |
| Mission San Juan Capistrano (1776) | Juaneño |
| Mission San Gabriel Archangel (1777) | Gabrielino |
| Mission San Fernando Rey de Espana (1797) | Fernandeño |

**Mid 19th Century Indian Names**

During the middle 19th century, the US Bureau of Indian Affairs (BIA) began the process of registering California Indian tribes as sovereign nations under then-existing USA-Indian treaties. Because Indian tribal boundaries in Southern California were ill defined, and because the state was so newly admitted to the Union (1850), the BIA simply lumped all Southern California Indians into one tribe, calling them "Mission Indians". Sub-groups such as Diegueños, Luiseños, etc were considered to be *Bands* (sometimes referred to as *tribelets)* of the major "Mission" tribe.

Even though most Indians native to Southern California have little or no connection to any of the old Spanish Catholic missions, they are still referred to as "Mission Indians". A case in point are the Serrano, Cahuilla, and Cupeño people. There never were Catholic missions in the territory claimed by the latter 3 groups, albeit there were small *Assistencias* (satellite sanctuaries). However, because theses people are located in Southern California the BIA simply includes them within the "Mission" tribe.

**Late 19th Century Indian Names**

Inasmuch as church related tribal names have been assigned to Indians by Non-Indians, many current Indian people do not choose to be called "Diegueño" or "Luiseño", or "Juaneño", etc. Early in California's history, Indian people from northern San Diego county referred to themselves as *IPAI (ee-pie)*, which can be translated in the Hokan language as meaning *"the people"*. Those Hokan speaking people from southern San Diego county called themselves *"TIPAI" (tee-pie)*, which means the same except in a different dialect. Those closely related Indian people living south of the international border called themselves *"Kumeyaay"*. They all, however, speak dialects of the Hokan language.

**Current Indian Names**

During the middle 19th century and into the last quarter of the 20th century, Southern California Indian tribes were severely decimated due to indenturing (buying and selling Indians people), racial biases, and economic handicaps. As a result, many Indians left their traditional cultures to meld into a Caucasian society, thus escaping the severe prejudices so rampant in Southern California. As a result, these Indian people faded into the racial melting pot and became simply *Urban Indians*. However, during the third and fourth quarters of the 20th century, Indians began reclaimed some of their heritage and culture due to economic gains afforded them through Indian Gaming. Many tribes are now devoting considerable attention to original tribal names, languages, and customs, thus trying to live down the Catholic mission-association names. For example, Indian people in northern Diegueño country refer to themselves as *Ipai*, rather than Diegueño. Many Gabrielino people prefer to be called *Tongva*, and the people formerly referred to as *Juaneños* call themselves *Achajemem*. When used in this treatise, the term *"Mission"*, or *"Mission Indian"*, capitalized and within quotation marks, refers to an Indian tribe. The word mission, sans quotation marks or capitalization, refers to church associated facilities and not to people. When associated with basketry, the term "Mission Basket" is capitalized and placed in quotation marks.

Prior to the latter quarter of the 20th century, those Hokan speaking people immediately south of the international border were referred to as *Kumeyaay* and those on the US side as *Tipai*. However, in the late 1900's anthropologists started referring to Tipai people in southern San Diego county as *"Kumeyaay"*, apparently because they and the Kumeyaay people of Baja California speak a somewhat similar tongue. By the start of the 21st century, this *"Kumeyaay"* moniker was spreading north and east at an alarming rate, to include the Ipai and Colorado River people. Many Non-Indians, and even some Indians, are jumping on the "name changing band wagon". Hopefully the fad will stop spreading before it reaches the Hokan speaking people called "Chumash", or "Yurok", "Atsugewi", or any of the numerous other Hokan speaking tribes of northern California. It has been jokingly claimed (by the author) that at the current rate of spread, all Indian people between the north pole and the Equator will soon be called *Kumeyaay*. Oh yes, one of the other justifications for this change of name by Non-Indians is that many Indians simply resent the church-related moniker. The author, being of Ipai heritage, fully understands this association and prefers to use the term Ipai (which is a Hokan word meaning "the people". If he holds any resentment, it is to those people who capriciously assign names to other people.

# CHAPTER 2

# "Mission" Indian Baskets

## Similarities In Materials

The territory generally associated with "Mission Indians" (please see the map, Figure 2, on the following page) is quite large: i.e. virtually all of Southern California, and geographically varies widely; Viz. from sea shore-to coastal plains-to high mountains (over 11,000 foot elevation)-to below sea level desert (elevation minus 200 feet). However, basketry produced by the various bands is remarkably similar. This is surprising, when it is recognized that there are two radically different linguistic families in the region, which suggest that the two groups had different cultural and geographic origins. It would seem logical to assume that people with different origins would have different basketry. That is, however, not necessarily the case with "Mission" people.

A discussion of "Mission Baskets" in general, should begin by discussing those characteristics that are similar, or nearly identical. In a later chapter, differences are discussed in more detail. Virtually all "Mission Baskets" are formed using the coiling technique, in which a foundation, or core, of plant fibers is wrapped by a stitching material, also of plant fibers, which sews one coil to the underlying coil.

## Plant Fibers

Perhaps the greatest basketry commonality in all of Southern California is the almost identical use of plant fibers. It can be said that virtually every "Mission Basket" contains at least one of the following plant materials:

**For the Coil Foundation,** one or a combination of:

Deer Grass seed stalks *(Muhlenbergia rigins)*
Deer Grass seed stalks are very long, slender, and covered with tiny seeds on the upper half, slightly resembling bristles on a brush. The stalk is usually 2 to 4 feet long, rarely more than 1/16 inch in diameter, is very rigid, and quite strong. Please see Figure 1 at right. Note the long slender seed stalks extend approximately 4 feet above the plant's leaves.

**Figure 1.** Deer Grass (*Muhlenbergia rigins*)

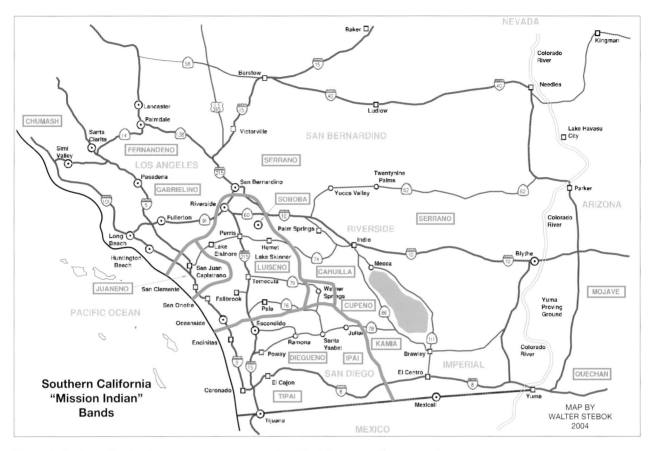

**Figure 2.** Southern California "Mission Indian" Bands

Split or shredded Juncus: *(Juncus sp.)*

In regions where Deer Grass was scarce, weavers occasionally used scrap Juncus weaver strands in their foundations. This is not a common practice because Deer Grass was found so readily in almost all climes. However, some weavers were apparently very frugal with their weaving materials or were unable to gather Deer Grass easily and thus used any foundation material available.

Whole Juncus rods: *(Juncus sp.)*

Chumash weavers frequently, and Gabrielino weavers occasionally, used a foundation composed of three small whole Juncus (*Juncus textilis or balticus*) reeds. Rarely is a 3-rod Juncus foundation found in any but Chumash or Gabrielino baskets.

**For Stitching Materials:**

Split Juncus *(Juncus textilis):*

Of the estimated 50 varieties of Juncus growing in California alone, only two were ever used, to any extent, for stitching material in Southern California; viz. *J. textilis* and *J. acutus. Juncus textilis* is by far the most common. It is a tall (4 to 8 foot) member of the Reed family that prefers either damp soil or canyon bottoms. When first harvested it is a deep forest green, which must be bleached to a buff, or sand, color usually by exposure to bright sun. After sun bleaching it is split longitudinally into very thin weavers strands and trimmed to the desired thinness.

Split Sumac: *(Rhus trilobata)*

There are a number of varieties of Rhus in Southern California. Rhus trilobata is a low growing shrub very similar to Poison Oak and grows in thickets similar to wild roses or a brier patch (see Figure 3). Two to four foot long switches of first year growth were harvested in the late Autumn or Winter, and split longitudinally (lengthwise) into thirds. The core and bark were removed and only the paper-thin *cambium* layer used as a stitching material; i.e. that layer just under the bark which carries the sap. This weaver strand was wrapped around the coil foundation and used to stitch, or bind, one coil to the preceding coil.

**Figure 3.** Sumac *(Rhus trilobata)* growing in a mature thicket

**For Pattern Materials:**

Natural basal red Juncus: *(Juncus textilis)*

This is the basal 6" to 12" portion of the reed that grows just below the dead thatch and soil layers. It is brownish-red in color and varies widely in hue and length. Basket makers used this basal part of the Juncus plant for creating their patterns motifs, so commonly seen in Diegueño and Serrano baskets. Luiseño weavers used basal red much less frequently for pattern motifs. Basal red Juncus varies widely in hue but can be used artistically to create a beautiful pattern, as seen in Figure 4.

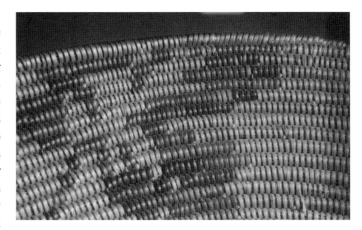

**Figure 4.** Basal red Juncus as used to create a pattern motif.

Dyed black Juncus: *(Juncus textilis.)*

Juncus weaver strands were frequently dyed black by: 1) emersion in a solution of rusty iron water and acorns (to add tannin), 2) burying Juncus strands in bay muds or near iron rich springs, 3) soaking in a solution of Elderberry blossoms and leaves, 4) soaking in hulls of native walnuts, or 5) various other methods. Commercial dyes were rarely, if ever used by California Indian basket makers.

Split Yucca root: *(Yucca brevifolia,* i.e. Joshua Tree)

Yucca root is a very striking material but was used only by those Indians living in or near the High Desert. Yucca roots are about the diameter of a wooden lead pencil and have an outer fleshy coating which must be stripped away, leaving a woody root which has a deep maroon-red outer surface and tan heart wood. The woody root is split longitudinally, similar to Sumac, and the core removed such that only the outer red material is used.

Commercial dyes:

Rarely did Southern California Indians use a commercial dye for pattern material. However, on rare occasions, when a natural color was unavailable, a basket maker used a rusty reddish brown dye, approximating the color of basal red Juncus. It can be detected by its consistent color over a long section of weaver strand, which is unobtainable with natural colors. Very rarely, a basket may be found with a vibrant red, or deep blue hue. These are presumably from commercial, or aniline dyes. Commercial dyes fade very quickly under direct sunlight so it is possible that some commercial dyes were used in very old baskets but faded into obscurity.

Natural Dyes:

Little has been recorded regarding use of natural or vegital dyes on basketry materials. The author has been told by several plant specialists that Durango Root, Indigo Bush, Dalea, etc, were used on rare occasions to dye basketry materials. However, little can be found in the literature regarding such uses, and even less evidence in actual baskets. The one exception is the processes employed to obtain a deep black.

Mr. George Wharton James, in his book *THROUGH RAMONA'S COUNTRY*, described a lavender color created by two Indian sisters; one from Warner's Hot Springs (Cupeño) and one from Mesa Grande (Ipai Diegueño). He described the color as resulting from soaking Juncus in Tule root juice. Such a basket, collected by George Wharton James, is in the basketry collection of the Pechanga Indian tribe. The lavender color has faded to almost an olive drab hue. The author previously owned another such basket in which the lavender color is very bright.

**Other Pattern Materials:**

Devils Claw: *(Myrtinia probosis)*

On rare occasions a "Mission Basket" may be found with materials other than those listed above. Devils claw is a low desert plant used extensively by Arizona and New Mexico Indians for black pattern elements. A "Mission Basket" containing Devils Claw is usually attributed to an Arizona Indian marrying into a "Mission" Indian family.

Pine Needles: *(Pinus coulterii)*

Occasionally a collector will happen upon a "Mission Basket" made of Pine Needles with split Juncus, or Sumac, stitching material. A controversy arises (sometimes heatedly) when students or collectors discuss Pine Needle Indian baskets; viz. are Pine Needles a true native basketry material, or was use of Pine Needles introduced by Non-Indians? The author **will *not go there***. It is, however, safe to say that Pine Needles were used only by a very small group of Indian weavers. Perhaps the best known of all Indian weavers using Pine Needles was the late Juanita Nejo Lopez. She was an Ipai lady who married Mr. Lopez, a member of the Pechanga Band and lived her married years on the Pechanga reservation. She made literally hundreds of Pine Needle baskets, including a number of such hats. The only other known Pine Needle users were members of the Osuna family near Santa Ysabel in San Diego County and an unnamed weaver in Mesa Grande. Non-Indian basket weavers make extensive use of Pine Needles in their basketry arts.

Raffia:

>Raffia is an imported plant-like material which has a waxy, crepe paper-like texture and is purchased in skeins much as one would buy yarn. It is used very extensively by Non-Indian weavers in a variety of arts and crafts. Because it is not an indigenous plant, California Indians (almost) never used it.

## Weaving Methods:

With but rare exceptions, all "Mission Baskets" were constructed using the *coiling* technique. In most cases Deer Grass seed stalks constitute the foundation material, about which strands of Juncus or Sumac were wrapped and then sewn to the underlying coil using a *pierce -penetrate - wrap* procedure. On rare occasions, a *throw-away* basket was constructed of whole Juncus reeds using an open twined technique (see basket A1-88 for an example). These are purely utilitarian baskets and were rarely saved after their initial use, let alone collected by serious collectors. Today, such baskets are highly sought after and, although not commanding a huge price, none-the-less fetch a very respectable price and are a welcome addition to any collection of "Mission Baskets".

## Bound Under Fag End Stitch (BUFES):

One of the important diagnostic traits of a "Mission Basket" is the *Bound Under Fag End Stitch (BUFES)*. By definition, a *fag end* is the beginning of a weaver strand and is on the end opposite the *running end*. The running end might be compared to the needle end of a needle and thread for darning socks (who darns socks anymore?). A BUFES is created by placing the equivalent of a half-hitch at the very beginning of the strand (the fag end) to keeps it from coming loose while tightening the initial stitch of that strand. A BUFES can be recognized in a basket as a very short (1/8" or less) stub sticking up and to the right at about 45 degrees from the coil. A master weaver keeps the stub very short, sometimes as short as 1/16". However, some weavers incorporate the fag stub into an innovative subtle pattern. Please see Figure 5.

Most "Mission" weavers use the BUFES almost exclusively. However, some Desert Cahuilla, Gabrielino, or Chumash weavers clip their fag ends flush with the surface. In the latter case, the weaver strand is technically not "clipped", it is twisted until it parts tight against the coil. Generally, however, presence of a BUFES is almost certain to signify a "Mission Basket".

**Figure 5.** Examples of Bound Under Fag End Stitch in third coil below the terminal. Another is immediately to the right of the dark pattern material. Note also the 15 back stitches on the terminal.

## Coil Direction:

Perhaps the most diagnostic Characteristic of a "Mission" basket is the direction of coil. Except in very rare cases, ***all "Mission Baskets" coil clockwise.*** Direction of coil can be determined almost instantly by looking at the slant of the stitches. If stitches slant **up and to the left**, as they do in Figure 5, the basket coils to the right, or clockwise; i.e. it is ***right handed***. If, however, they slant up and to the right, then it coils counterclockwise, or left handed. It matters not whether the basket is viewed from the *work or non-work* side, nor whether the weaver was right or left handed. The *work side* is the side where the weaver's awl penetrated the coil. The *non-work side* is where the awl emerged on the back side of the coil. When a ***right handed*** basket is viewed from the *work side*, the terminal will point to the right, as in Figure 5.

It is questionable whether 1% of all "Mission Baskets" coil left handed. In other words, perhaps 99% of all "Mission" baskets coil right handed.

**Basket Shapes:**

Inasmuch as baskets were originally used for virtually all household purposes, they were made in a wide variety of sizes and shapes, depending upon their intended function. After about the last quarter of the 19th century, most Southern California Indians abandoned their traditional uses of basketry, having adopted metal or glass containers, *like the White Guys do*! There was, therefore, a general hiatus in basket creation during the middle to late 1800's. However, beginning circa 1880–1890, Non-Indians began collecting local baskets as ethnic art pieces or as remnants of a culturally endangered art form. Indian ladies were very quick to realize that an Indian basket was no longer an *implement*, it was a *commodity*. ERGO, a *cottage industry* was born and by about 1900, Indian basket weavers were beginning to realize cash for their art work. Unfortunately, many of the new weavers were more interested in selling a basket than they were in retaining authenticity. Shapes suddenly became dictated by what sold best. Some weavers clung to their traditional shapes but many did not. It is therefore not a safe bet to assign a given shape to a given tribe, EXCEPT in certain cases where a shape became almost diagnostic of a given weaver or territory; e.g. the famous *Soboba bowl* and the less famous *spittoon* shaped bowl from the so-called *spittoon-belt*.

By way of explanation, many post 1900 weavers on the Soboba reservation seemed to favor a small bowl which bellied out dramatically very low on the sides. Although Soboba had a hybrid of Luiseño, Serrano and Cahuilla weavers, many apparently adopted this *low belly* shape.

The above mentioned *Spittoon belt* is a geographical corridor that extends from the Jacumba region in southeastern San Diego County, then northwesterly to Lake Cuyamaca, to Santa Ysabel, and into the Hemet/Soboba area. S*emi-spittoon* shaped baskets from this *belt* are bowls in which the neck appears to have been stretched upward and slightly outward. Such shaped baskets are almost always traceable to this *spittoon belt*.

***Esperanza Sobenish, a close-up of her starting a basket***

Mr. Edward Davis captured Mrs. Esperanza Sobenish on film in 1919 on the Rincon reservation as she began creating a large flat bottom basket. Apparently Mr. Davis, on the same visit, also took photographs of Mrs. Sobenish working on a large basket with a rattlesnake design. An original print of this photograph was given to the author by Mrs. Ann Davis, Edward Davis' granddaughter.

# CHAPTER 3

# *Luiseño Baskets And Their Characteristics*

## Geography

Geography and plant occurrences in Luiseño tribal territory are discussed in detail elsewhere in this treatise. Suffice it to say at this point that much of Luiseño territory is located in Southern California's coastal plains. Sumac and Deer Grass are found at numerous locations and are relatively plentiful. Juncus, on the other hand, is found in limited quantities at only scattered locations. Current steps are being initiated in Orange County by basketry students, Indians, and botanists to study relationship between topography, soil conditions, and characteristics of the basal red portion of Juncus reeds. At this time, the consensus seems to be that coastal plains Juncus does not attain the quality found in the more mountainous regions. This is born out by the fact that most Luiseño baskets do not exhibit extensive red pattern motifs, as compared with Diegueño, or Serrano baskets. Nor do they exhibit the generous use of both basal red and dyed black Juncus so common to Cahuilla or Serrano baskets. Where basal red pattern material is used by Luiseños, it's hue is often rather subdued and secondary to dyed black Juncus motifs.

## Sumac Versus Juncus

It was stated in personal conversation with Julia Parker, a master basket creator in Yosemite, and a basketry student of the author, that preparation of a Sumac weaver strand takes from 3 to 5 times as long as does a Juncus strand. Experience proves that most Sumac weaver strands end up somewhat shorter than Juncus strands because of breakage during core or bark removal. As a result, weaving with Sumac weaver strands take much longer than with strands of Juncus.

As for total time required to complete a basket, some weavers contend that it takes approximately as long to prepare a Juncus weaver strand, ready for weaving, as it does to actually weave that strand into a basket. For example, if a basket maker spends 100 hours actually weaving a specific Juncus basket (not an unreasonable amount of time), then another 100 hours must be spent gathering, curing, splitting, trimming, and sizing the weaving materials. This equates to a total 200 hours expended to create a specific basket. If a Sumac strand takes 3 times as long to prepare as a Juncus strand, then it follows, logically, that the same size basket, made entirely of Sumac takes approximately 400 hours; i.e. $100 + (100 \times 3) = 400$ hours, or twice as long as with Juncus. It therefore takes no stretch of the fleshy tablets of the mind to understand why Juncus was a much preferable material to use when completion time was critical, as was the case in a great many baskets created for sale. Unfortunately, good quality

Juncus is not nearly as durable as is Sumac. Therefore, if a basket was made for utility purposes, the weaver would more wisely invest her time using Sumac in preference to Juncus.

**Dyed Juncus versus Dyed Sumac**

One of the more favorable characteristics of Juncus is that it takes, and retains, a stain or dye much more readily than does Sumac. One of the more common dye colors used in Luiseño baskets is black, which is relatively easy to achieve. Prior to subjecting a weaver strand to dying, it is first split and trimmed to a desired width. It is then subjected to one of the following procedures:

* ❖ buried in lake shore or ocean bay muds, or
* ❖ buried in muds at a water source (spring or stream) which is rich in iron, or
* ❖ soaked in a rusty water solution to which acorns (tannin) have been added, or
* ❖ soaked in a solution of Elderberry leaves, fruit , or blossoms, or
* ❖ soaked in a solution of wild Black Walnut hulls and acorns, or
* ❖ soaked in a solution of any number of other plants.

The amount of time required to achieve the desired black color varies with the method. Rarely, however, can a satisfactory hue be achieved in less than several weeks. The dying process is not only long, it is also smelly, accompanied by odors, gnats, flies, and other less than desirable flying, walking, or crawling critters. Quite obviously, a basket maker does not resort to a dying process if a pleasing and an acceptable natural colored material is available, such as basal red Juncus. Often, however, an acceptable basal red color is not available on Juncus within the coastal plains. It is therefore understanding why Luiseño weavers used colors sparingly in their design patterns by minimizing the size, design, or nature of their pattern motifs.

Inasmuch as Sumac does not readily accept, and retain a dye, it was rarely colored, either with vegetal or commercial dyes.

**Pattern Motifs**

Virtually all "Mission Baskets" were made in much the same way, with much the same materials, and using much the same weaving techniques. However, each band, or sub-band followed certain tribal pattern styles, which seem to be almost diagnostic for that band. For example, Cahuilla baskets can be summarized as being very colorful and *busy*, with generous use of anthropomorphs (stylized humans), zoomorphs (stylized animals), or stylized natural phenomenon (whirl wind, comet, stars, etc.). Dyed black Juncus was used to complement dark basal red Juncus pattern elements. On the other hand Diegueño baskets made very little use of dyed black Juncus, using instead generous amounts of vivid basal red Juncus as a pattern material, creating geometric forms such as triangles, rectangles, diamonds, or stars. Rarely were natural phenomenon, zoomorphic or anthropomorphs pattern motifs used by Diegueño weavers.

Luiseño baskets, by comparison, are quite subdued in pattern and make use of black dyed Juncus with minimal use of basal red pattern elements. Unlike other "Mission Baskets", many by Luiseño weavers contain one or several narrow black horizontal band on their sides. With certain exceptions, pattern motifs are mostly horizontally oriented and geometric in form, with few zoomorphic, anthropomorphic, or natural phenomenon motifs. Exceptions to the above are generally area-specific, such as at Soboba or Pechanga, which are discussed in greater detail in a later chapter but mentioned below in broad terms.

**Soboba Baskets**

An interesting cultural anomaly occurred during the latter years of the 19th century at Soboba, which is located only a dozen miles northeast of Hemet in Riverside County. This reservation, which was established in 1883 by the US Congress, is located well within Cahuilla geographical territory. In fact, Soboba is located many miles away from what is today considered Luiseño territory. When establishing Indian reservations during the middle-late 19ᵗʰ century, the Bureau of Indian Affairs (BIA) did not consider a specific band as having any established tribal territory. The BIA's primary concern was to find a tract of land which could be obtained by the government and upon which they could relocate Indians, regardless of ethnic, cultural, or linguistic affiliations.

Inasmuch as tribal lands between Banning and Temecula were well suited for agriculture and cattle range, it was in high demand by Non-Indian Americans. Thus was raised the age-old conflict between Indians and Non-Indians regarding land ownership. As might be expected, Indians were removed from their ancestral homes and moved into a common reservation with all other Indians living within the region. Such land was neither wanted nor useful to Anglo farmers or cattlemen. Soboba was selected because it was neither desirable for agriculture nor cattle raising. Although most of the Indians located at Soboba spoke a dialect of the Uto-Aztecan (Shoshonean) language, their ancestral origins differed widely. Families from what are now known as Cahuilla, Serrano, Luiseño, Gabrielino, and even a few Diegueño were relocated into one reservation and expected to live as one big happy family, even though many did not share a common language.

Even though Soboba people are native to the Riverside-San Bernardino region, their basketry differs, sometimes dramatically from other Bands. Many pre-1900 baskets tend to show Pass Cahuilla traits, while others resemble classic Luiseño styles. Interestingly enough, a sort of hybrid design/shape evolved from weavers at this specific reservation. This hybrid design manifested itself primarily in bowls, gift baskets, and globular baskets created for the tourist trade.

Most globular "Mission Baskets" tend to have a uniform, consistent curve, when viewed from the side, with their widest diameter approximately midway between the rim and the base. Not so with many Soboba baskets! When making one of these baskets some Soboba weavers placed the widest diameter at the *belly,* well below its midpoint, which gave the basket a "squat" or *pear* shape. To complicate this design, the neck, or mouth did not necessarily curve uniformly inward. Instead, the rim often curved slightly upward, rather than inward, which gave the basket what might be described as a *stretched neck.*

A more detailed description of Soboba baskets is included in a later chapter, wherein a number of Soboba baskets are described in detail.

## Pechanga Baskets

Although many Luiseño basket patterns are considered rather austere, with dyed black Juncus the predominant pattern material, such is not the case with some Pechanga weavers. Prior to the land boom near Temecula in the latter quarter of the 20th century, there was a small group of ladies residing in this Temecula Valley who were extraordinary basket makers. Unfortunately, few baskets created by these ladies have survived into the 21st century. The Riverside Municipal Museum (RMM) collection contains only 5 baskets attributed to a Pechanga weaver. These five were all collected by Mr. Harwood Hall, a former superintendent at Sherman Institute in Riverside. All five are exceedingly fine baskets and created in the style of Cahuilla *fancy baskets*. These baskets are described and photographed in Chapter 9 page 61.

Surprisingly, the Riverside Municipal Museum collection contains few, if any baskets by Mrs Juanita Nejo Lopez who made literally hundreds of Pine Needle baskets. Unfortunately, Pine Needle baskets were not popular during the early-middle 20th century, so few appear in museum collections. Inasmuch as there are no Juanita Nejo baskets pictured in the catalogue, a description of her basketry is in order at this point. Her baskets are rather unique and quite easy to recognize, in that:

❖ They all incorporate Pine Needles in their foundation
❖ Pine Needle fascicles (paper-like covering of the needle's base) were used to create design motifs,
❖ All have a flat base and vertical sides
❖ The "start" is composed of almost pure white Sumac wrapping a cordage foundation
❖ After approximately 3 revolutions of white Sumac and cordage foundation, she shifted to Juncus stitching over a foundation of Pine Needles.
❖ Her hats are also of Pine Needles and are fashioned after straw hats worn at the start of the 1900's

# CHAPTER 4

# Luiseño Territory vs. Basketry

## Tribal Boundaries

Luiseño people occupy that part of the California coastal plain generally from the region just south of Oceanside, north to the canyon opposite San Onofre, and inland for 10 to 30 miles. The Luiseño-Diegueño frontier, just south of Oceanside, is fairly well defined because the two bands speak an entirely different language; the Diegueños speak a *Hokan* based tongue, while Luiseños speak a dialect of *"Uto-Aztecan"*, aka *"Shoshonean"*. To the north and east, Luiseño boundaries are more loosely delineated because the Shoshonean language is also spoken by abutting tribes. At the Chumash/Gabrielino frontier around Malibu, a dialect of the *Hokan* language is spoken, somewhat akin to that of the Diegueños.

Luiseño territory starts at the ocean south of Oceanside and extends generally northeast bordering the San Luis Rey River canyon, then easterly paralleling that canyon to Lake Henshaw, then generally northwesterly along California State Route 79 to approximately Aguanga, then north toward Hemet, then westerly generally following State Route 74 to Lake Elsinore and over the mountains, back to the coast in the vicinity of San Onofre (where the electrical generating plant is located). This fairly large tract is rather steeply rolling with extensive brush fields. Only in the Mount Palomar Mountains and in the Mountains west of Lake Elsinore are there any timber lands or does the terrain get into the "mountainous" category.

These people are bordered on the north by Juaneño and Gabrielino (Tongva), on the east by Cahuilla, at one point by the Cupeño (former at Warner's Hot Springs), and on the south by Diegueños (Ipai).

## Luiseño Sub-tribes ("Tribelets")

Within the Luiseño region, the US Bureau of Indian Affairs (BIA) established, and recognizes five Indian reservations; viz. Rincon, La Jolla, Pauma, Pala, and Pechanga. In addition, there is a sizable number of Luiseño families living on the reservation at Soboba, which is technically in Cahuilla country. A seventh enclave (not a recognized reservation) exists near Mission San Luis Rey, east of Oceanside. While all seven *"Bands"* speak a common Shoshonean base language, there are enough differences that each might be called a dialect.

Because each sub-band inhabits slightly different geographic areas, with differing climatic conditions and vegetation, it is not unreasonable to find that their basketry varies slightly. In addition, because many basket makers learned the art form and styles from their elders, it is only natural that certain characteristics emerged, distinguishing one sub-band from another. In some anthropological circles, these smaller entities are referred to as *"tribelets"*.

# CHAPTER 5

# *Basketry Characteristics*

## Impetus For RMM's Exhibit

D
r. H. Vincent Moses, in his introduction hereto, stated that Dr. Christopher Moser, the museum's late Curator of Anthropology, worked tirelessly to interest the US Postal Service in commemorating the exceptionally fine art displayed in basketry of the Southern California Indian, particularly those of the Luiseño band of "Mission Indians". Depiction of one such Indian art piece on a US Postal Service stamp in August 2004, therefore, offered the impetus for mounting an exhibit of some of the Luiseño baskets in the RMM (Riverside Municipal Museum) collection. Available floor space limited the museum to only a portion of RMM's rather substantial collection of Indian baskets. It did, however, create a golden opportunity to make an in-depth study of Luiseño basket characteristics. Inasmuch as each basket was closely inspected, as well as photographed by the author, it was a simple matter to develop a format whereby each basketry characteristics could be arrayed such that the preponderance of traits could be displayed graphically.

## Individual Characteristics

In order that each basket might be classified as to its individual characteristics, a list of 60 basketry details was prepared. Each basket was carefully inspected and its various characteristics were noted, as depicted in Table 1, page 77, in the SUMMARY chapter. The presence, or absence, of each characteristic was noted for every basket in the exhibit. It is hoped that a careful scrutiny of that summary table will assist the serious student in defining parameters of Luiseño baskets, and show variations in styles, shapes, materials, and patterns.

During the course of these inspections and analyses, it was obvious that all Luiseño baskets in this exhibit, except one, are of the coiled style; i.e. they were created by sewing a stitching material (Sumac or Juncus weaver strands) around a long rope-like bundle of fibrous material, either Deer Grass seed-stalks or split Juncus. That foundation spirals outward from its "start" to its terminal at the final end. Inasmuch as virtually all "Mission Baskets" are of this coiling style, and because virtually all foundations coil clockwise (right handed), these two features are taken for granted and not noted in the tables.

## Summary Bar Chart

After completion of all descriptions, a summary bar chart was prepared and is included as Table 1 in the SUMMARY chapter. The purpose of that bar chart is to graphically illustrate the preponderance of characteristics; i.e. what are the generic characteristics of a Luiseño basket. For example, it was noted that of the three different types of *"starts"*, *the Bent Finger and Pierced Wad* were equally popular (38% each) but the *Knot* type (18%) was not a favorite. The chart does, however show a very clear preference for a Deer Grass seed stalk *"start"* foundation over use of Yucca fibers, which are very frequently used by other "Mission Indian" weavers. The chart also shows that the vast majority of baskets contain a preponderance of dyed black Juncus (95%), rather than basal red Juncus (19%) for pattern material. Selection of dyed black over natural basal red Juncus was discussed in a previous chapter.

**A Word of Caution** is deemed appropriate at this point. Data and information inscribed on the nine tables in the appendix hereto were gleaned from an inspection of baskets in the RMM collection only. Of those baskets included in this catalogue 33%, were collected by Mr. and Mrs. Cornelius Rumsey circa 1900. Another 23% were collected by Harwood Hall, also circa 1900, and 19% were collect by Mr and Mrs Frank Miller, again circa 1900. In other words, 75% of all Luiseño baskets discussed herein were obtained by only three collectors, most of which predate 1900. It can probably be said that both Cornelius Rumsey and Harwood Hall had certain favorite styles or patterns which dictated the style of baskets they acquired, while the Frank Millers were collecting baskets to display in their *Mission Inn.* It is therefore reasonable to assume that the details described in these tables reflect the likes and dislikes of only these three collectors. On the other side of the coin, these three collectors were active around, or before the turn of the 20th century so the baskets thus collected were created prior to the on-rush of tourists during the 1900 to 1930 basketry renaissance. These baskets, therefore, only minimally reflect tourist influences in design and styles. The readers attention is directed to the paragraph entitled "Unintentional Bias" in Chapter 10 which discusses bias on the part of collectors.

It is hoped that a careful use of the attached tables will enable some basketry students to better understand Luiseño baskets, both before and after the basket renaissance.

***Doloras (Roderiquez) (sic); lady in white making a small basketry tray***

This photograph was reproduced from an original photograph taken in July, 1930, by Edward Davis of Mesa Grande, California. An original of that print was given to the author by Mrs. Ann Davis, granddaughter of Edward Davis. A caption on the photo jacket reads "Doloras (sic) making a basket, July 1930 Mesa Grande, Calif. The name "Roderiquez" (sic) was written later.

CHAPTER 6

# *Definition of Terms Used Herein (Glossary)*

In the course of assessing and describing the subject basketry collection, a number of terms were used, or coined (for this treatise) by the author. Customarily, when esoteric terms are used they are included in a glossary in the back matter of a book, where few people ever explore. When so located, a reader first encounters a word or term with an unknown meaning. That reader must then abandon the text, initiate a search *somewhere* trying to locate the glossary and determine the word's meaning, then go back to the text and try to remember what caused the interruption in the first place and pick up the scattered pieces of a thought train.

In this treatise, word or term meanings are hopefully explained before the reader encounters them in the text, which obviates the frantic search and a break in the thought process.

**Anomaly:** An intentional pattern break, created by inserting a foreign or incongruous motif. It can be a minor change in size or shape, or it can be a substantially different motif, obviously placed by the weaver for no discernable reason.

**Anthropomorphic:** Any pattern element that can be construed as being a stylized human.

**Back Stitch:** After the terminal is completed, some weavers continue stitching but reverse direction, climbing back up onto the foundation away from the terminal, creating a pseudo herringbone stitch.

**Band:** A series of red or black stitches no more than several coils wide, running horizontally around a basket.

**Basket Renaissance:** The period generally from 1890 to 1930, when making Indian baskets for sale became a major cottage industry. Literally thousands were made, and sold, during this time period. However, styles and patterns were often dictated by what sold best, not by tradition.

**"Bent Finger" Start:** A "start" created by wrapping an elongated bundle of fibers with Juncus or Sumac and then bending that wrapped bundle back onto itself, much like bending the index finger when making a fist, after which the sides are stitched together to create an oval shaped "start".

**Block:** A generally square, boldly colored rectangle that creates a negative motif on the inside, such as a *Vee, Diamond, Deer Track, Circle, Rectangle,* etc.

**"BUFES":** An acronym using the first letter of **B**ound **U**nder **F**ag **E**nd **S**titch. The fag end of a weaver strand is the beginning or lower end as opposed to the *running, or needle end.*

**Clipped Fag End:** When starting a new weaver strand, some weavers leave about 1 inch of the fag end sticking out. After it has dried several days, the basket is held firm and the weaver strand is twisted until it ruptures at the point of emergence from the foundation.

**Clockwise:** The direction of a basket's coil indicates how stitching progresses. Direction of coil is always determined with reference to the *work side.* If the direction is clockwise (aka *right handed),* the stitches will slant **up** and to the **left** A counter clockwise stitch (left handed) will slant **up** and to the **right.**

**Coil:** A rope-like portion of the basket, which extends one complete 360 degree revolution. That coil is sewn to the previous coil via a weaver strand.

**Concave:** An upward curve in the basket's bottom; i.e. upward into the basket, as viewed from the top looking down.

**Concentric:** One motif placed inside another of the same type.

**Convex:** A down-curving of a basket's bottom; i.e curving downward away from the basket, as contrasted to CONCAVE.

**Enclosed By Band:** A pattern or series of motifs with a band at the top and bottom, thus enclosing that pattern or motifs.

**Fag End:** The blunt, beginning end of a weaver strand, which is opposite the running or pointed end.

**Floral:** A motif that resembles a plant, tree, leaf, or flower.

**Foundation:** The central part of a basket's coil. When used in coiled basketry, the foundation resembles a long slender rope about which either Sumac or Juncus is stitched (wrapped).

**Gift Basket:** A small globular basket usually made to be given as a gift. Workmanship was usually very good. Many baskets made during the basket renaissance were of this type.

**Grass:** *Grass* is a corruption of a common name for *Muhlenbergia rigens,* aka *Deer Grass, Clump Grass, or Bunch Grass,* all of which are proper names. The usable part is the long (24" to 48") slender fruit or seed stalk, from which the seeds had been stripped. The stalk is normally about 1/16 to 1/8 inch in diameter but very rigid.

**Horizontal:** A series of motifs arranged such that they are generally side-by-side, albeit not necessarily touching, and wrapping around the basket's side.

**Isolated:** Pattern motifs that do not touch, or are not arranged in any regular order.

**Joined:** A series of geometric forms or motifs connected by a line or touching on one or both sides.

**Juncus:** A weaver strand of the outer surface of a reed *Juncus textilis or Juncus sp (species unspecified).*

**Knot Start:** A "start" created by tying an overhand knot in a very flexible bundle of fibers, such as those from Yucca or Agave leaves, then stitching either Sumac or Juncus around, and through the knot's center hole creating what is sometimes called a *rosette.* It differs from a *Bent Finger* or *Pierced Wad* "start" by being more regular and consistent in shape and appearance.

**Lightning:** A slender nearly vertical *zig zag* motif shaped such as to conjure up a bolt of lightning in the viewer's mind.

**Negative Pattern:** A pattern created by outlining it with a contrasting color, such that a viewer sees the *inside* as the motif, not the colored portion; e.g. the **T** inside the star on Texaco's gasoline logo.

**Non-work Side:** The face of a basket opposite the *work side;* i.e. the basket's surface where the awl's point emerges, as contrasted to where the awl penetrates. Unless a weaver is very careful, location and angle of emergence is difficult to control, which means the non-work side is usually less orderly and neat than is the work side.

*Pierced Wad* **Start:** A "start" created by squeezing together a mass (wad) of flexible fibers and then encircling the entire mass with weaver strands, thus creating a network of rather random stitches.

**Provenance:** (Sometimes spelled *provenience)* Information as to the weaver's name, the weaver's tribe or origin, when or where it was collected, or any other relevant information.

**Rectangles:** A four sided geometric shape having its top and bottom parallel, and its two ends parallel and 90 degrees to the top and bottom. It may be longer than tall or vice versa, or it may be a perfect square.

**Running End:** That part of a weaver strand that is sharpened to a point and repeatedly penetrates the coil. The running end is opposite the fag end of a weaver strand.

**Spiral Blocks:** Any series of 3 or more blocks that rise in a stair-step fashion, either up-to the right, or up-to the left.

**Stacked:** One pattern motif placed on top of another of the same shape; e.g. a triangle sitting on top of another triangle.

**Stair Step**: A series of rectangles either rising or falling, as do steps in a stair case.

**"Start":** That part of the basket's very beginning including one whorl (revolution) or it may refer to several of the first whorls. It is placed in parentheses to distinguish the noun from a verb.

**Sumac:** A weaver strand composed of the cambium layer of a bush-like plant, *Rhus trilobata.* Some older sources refer to the plant as *Squaw Bush.* The word *"Squaw"* is a derogatory corruption of a Great Lakes Indian word referring to a lady's genitals, and should be stricken from the readers vocabulary.

**Tall:** A generally rectangular motif, noticeably taller than it is wide.

**Terminal:** The final end of the foundation on the outer rim of a basket. It is usually pointed and tapers from its full diameter to a point, usually within no more than several inches.

**Vertical:** A series of motifs arranged such that they extend from, or near, the basket's rim and reach to, or near, its bottom. They need not touch or be continuous.

**Weaver Strand:** A long, thin weaving element, usually of Juncus or Sumac, which is wrapped around the foundation and then used to sew one coil to an underlying coil.

**Whorl:** Same as a coil; i.e. a 360 degree turn in a foundation.

**Work Side:** The side of a basket into which the weaver inserts the awl and the strand's running end. Normally the weaver has good control over where, how, and what angle the awl enters the foundation on the *work side*. Less control is exerted over where the awl exists the non-work side. As a consequence the *work side* is usually much neater than is the *non-work side*. The work side may be on the inside or the outside, depending upon the basket's shape and which side the weaver wanted the basket to be viewed.

**Worm:** A small short motif that is horizontal, then steps up to another small horizontal element, similar to one short stair step.

**Zig Zag:** A motif that resembles a lightning bolt but composed of broader stair step rectangles ascending or descending.

**Zoomorphic:** A pattern motif depicting an animal, bird, insect or reptile.

# CHAPTER 7

# *Generic Luiseño Baskets*

### Basket Descriptions

In the introduction to this catalogue, Dr. H. Vincent Moses stated that one of the baskets in the RMM collection was featured in a US Postal Service stamp pane issued in August, 2004. To commemorate that issue, the Museum's staff mounted an exhibition of some of the Luiseño baskets in RMM's collection. Floor space at the museum, however, limited the number of such baskets which could be placed on public display. In the pages which follow, seventy-six Luiseño baskets are illustrated. An attempt was made herein to discuss relevant features of each basket which may not be visible in the photographs; e.g. date of collection or creation, name of the collector, history of the basket, etc. Space to fully discuss all basket personalities is also limited in this treatise. Never-the-less, when any information is salient, an attempt was made to provide that information.

For those interested in technical characteristics that may not be clearly visible in the photos, such as the nature of the "start", the terminal, back stitches, etc, a list was prepared of those features, and included in a tabular format. Nine such tables appear in the appendix hereto and includes each basket, by its museum accession number. A total of 60 individual traits are included. If the trait is present in a specific basket, an "X" appears in the table. Inasmuch as patterns and details of shape are reasonably visible in the photos, no attempt was made to describe them further in the tables.

The reader's attention is called to Table 1, page 77. The purpose of Table 1 is to show graphically which characteristics are most common in Luiseño baskets. Attention is also directed to the fact that every basket was individually created and thus reflects what the weaver wished to portray, not necessarily what the reader wishes to interpret. Even though this summary table may suggest that many Luiseño baskets have a certain trait, that does not suggest that ALL, or even most, Luiseño basket have that trait.

By way of explanation, the "A" in RMM's accession number refers to "Accession through gift". The second number identifies the specific donor; e.g. A1 denotes items donated by Mr. and Mrs. Cornelius Earle Rumsey. The third number defines the specific item in that accession package; e.g. A1-82 translate into the 82nd item donated by Mr. and Mrs. Cornelius Rumsey.

Please note that in a former chapter, a statement was made that 75% of all baskets considered in this treatise were collected by just three persons around the year 1900. Quite obviously, most collectors have certain preferences and baskets so acquired may reflect those preferences. Please note that the author also has biases which may have crept into the assessment. Therefore, the reader's attention is directed to discussion of Unintentional Bias in Chapter 10.

All photography of RMM baskets was by the author. Photos are reproduced herein courtesy of the Riverside Municipal Museum. When inquiring about a specific basket, contact the Museum's Curator of Collections and make reference to the accession number.

## RMM A1-7 (U2021) Shallow Tray

Most basketry students refer to any basket that is relatively flat, with virtually no vertical sides, as a tray. It need not have a perfectly flat bottom but should not be noticeably concave or convex. The subject basket is 13.5 inches in diameter, 3.5 inches deep, with a flat 6 inch diameter center, and is dated circa 1880's. This basket had, at one time, been taken from the collection and a lesser quality basket inserted with an A1-7 number. When this basket was returned, the number U2021 assigned. Later the original number was restored.

Pattern motifs are of dyed black Juncus. Negative spiraling "V's" in a black block ("deer hooves") are rather common Luiseño and Cahuilla motifs. Background ("field")material is split Sumac over a Deer Grass foundation which coils clockwise. Its "start" is a form of *knot* using Sumac over Deer Grass tips. There are horizontal bands of black Juncus near the bottom and near the rim.

RMM A1-7 Southern Luiseño Tray
Also pictured as Figure 15, page 16, *Rods, Bundles, and Stitches*

RMM A1-39 Southern Luiseño Bowl
Also pictured as Figure 220, page 119, *Native American Basketry of Southern California*

## RMM A1-39 Southern Luiseño Bowl

Mr. Rumsey collected this basket circa 1890 or earlier, with severe rim damage. Although pattern motifs differ somewhat, there are similarities between this and basket RMM A1-7; i.e. there are negative vertical lines in a connected series of black blocks. It does not, however, contain the black Juncus bands so common to Luiseño baskets. The basic stitching material is Sumac over a Deer Grass foundation. Fag ends are bound under.

Although museum records list this as a bowl, it is also listed as a parching tray. Most western US Indians parched their seeds by placing then in a relatively flat tray, together with several red hot wood coals, and then the mass was swirled so as to keep the tray from scorching but yet toast the seeds. Normally such trays exhibit at least a modicum of scorch marks. No such scorch marks are visible on this basket.

RMM A1-41 Luiseño Style Tray
Also pictured as Figure 122, page 71, *Native American Basketry of Southern California*

## RMM A1-41 Luiseño Gambling Tray

Dr. Christopher Moser, in his book, *Native American Basketry of Southern California,* listed this book as being in the Luiseño *"style"*. Most Luiseño baskets do not exhibit as elaborate a pattern as does this one, which resembles that by a Cahuilla weaver. However, most Cahuilla baskets use much more red/black pattern motifs, as compared with this early 1900's basket.

The basket is 15 inches in diameter and listed as a *Gambling Tray.* Prior to c. 1930's, Indians used trays such as this in their dice games, which were primarily a lady's activities. A bent finger start of Sumac over Yucca fibers began the coiling, with Sumac as a primary stitching material over a clockwise Deer Grass foundation. Pattern elements are in dyed black Juncus. Note the symmetrical design motifs. The rim terminal tapers gradually with 2 back stitches.

## RMM A1-50 Luiseño Shallow Bowl

A museum accession tag reads *"Riverside Indian"* for this circa 1900 12+ inches open bowl. It also has a "?" after the tribal name suggesting that its tribal origin is in question. That is perhaps because the design closely resemble those sometimes associated with Juaneño baskets; i.e. its motifs are vertically oriented, so commonly associated with Juaneño baskets. Stitching material is split Sumac, with a foundation of Deer Grass. Its 6 vertical rectangular elements are outlined with red Juncus, which is not a common Luiseño trait.

This open bowl has a *pierced wad* "start" of Sumac over a foundation of mixed Deer Grass tips and Yucca fibers. It coils clockwise and has a rather blunt rim terminal with 5 back stitches. There is a possibility that the weaver was of Juaneño heritage.

RMM A1-50 Luiseño Shallow Bowl
Also shown on Figure 272, page 140, *Rods, Bundles, and Stitches*

RMM A1-52 Luiseño Open Bowl
Also pictured as Figure 22, page 19, *Rods, Bundles, and Stitches*

## RMM A1-52 Luiseño Open Bowl

This rather crudely made basket was collected circa 1900 by Cornelius Rumsey. Although workmanship is less than perfect, its overall construction is somewhat typical of a Luiseño weaving; i.e. split Sumac over a Deer Grass foundation that coils clockwise. The weaver used a *pierced wad* "start" of Sumac over Deer Grass tips. She also included a single black band at the top of the pattern motifs that are described herein as a series of *fat H's with feet*. In most Luiseño baskets, where the band is connected to a design element, that band is at the element's base, not the top. The isolated "H" motifs are also rather unique. The weaver placed 4 black and 2 red isolated "worm" shaped figures near the rim, which is also rather atypical. Spacing of these *worm-like* figures is not uniform. The terminal is abrupt with no back stitches.

## RMM A1-54 Large Luiseño Shallow Basin

A comparison may be made between this and basket RMM A1-52, above. Both are open bowl/basins, both are composed primarily of split Sumac over a Deer Grass foundation that coils clockwise, both have isolated pattern motifs, and both have a horizontal dyed black Juncus band. The primary difference is that this basket has two horizontal black bands enclosing the pattern motifs, which is generally considered diagnostic for Luiseño baskets. Its terminal is rather blunt with 8 back stitches. An interesting feature of this pattern is that two of the motifs differ from the other four. This difference was referred to as a *pattern anomaly* in a video-taped lecture by Justin Farmer to the California Indian Arts Association in 1999.

Like the previous basket, this was collected by Cornelius Rumsey circa 1900.

RMM A1-54 Luiseño Shallow Basin
As illustrated in Figure 21, page 19, *Rods, Bundles, and Stitches*

## RMM A1-55 Luiseño Open Basin

Although the pattern on this bowl is quite plain, it could be described as having *simple elegance*. It has a 15 inch rim, is 5 inches deep, and is composed of virtually all split Sumac over a clockwise foundation of Deer Grass. Its "start" is of the *knot* style using Sumac over tips of Deer Grass. The weaver very artistically created two black and one red Juncus concentric 4 pointed stars, or flower petals. Please note that this weaver was very experienced and able to execute sides of the star in gentle curves which compliment the overall curvature of the bowl. On first blush, this sounds easy. However, it can be done, well, only after years of experience.

There are no black bands here, although the weaver accomplished a comparable effect using simple black lines on the star. Approximately one inch has been added to the top of this basket, which could be an old rim repair or perhaps it was sold before it was completed and finished later.

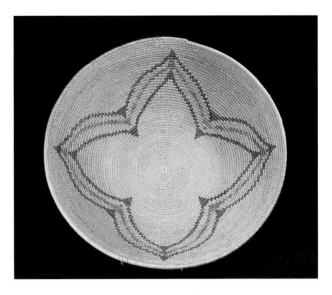

RMM A1-55 Luiseño Large Open Basin
Also displayed as Figure 18, page 18, *Rods, Bundles, and Stitches*

RMM A1-56 Luiseño Shallow Bowl
As seen in Figure 31, page 24, *Rods, Bundles, and Stitches*

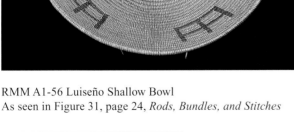

## RMM A1-56 Luiseño Shallow Bowl

Museum records indicate this circa 1900 basket to be a *"Luiseño- possibly Diegueño"* Shallow bowl. The *"possible* Diegueño" designation is apparently based upon use of Sumac over Yucca cordage for its *bent finger* "start". Use of Yucca fibers in its "start" is a questionable criterion. The pattern suggests a very possible Juaneño origin.

It is the author's belief that there are only several dozen Juaneño baskets extant with good provenance. Those that have been identified seem to have pattern much like this one; i.e. isolated simple geometric motifs arranged horizontally but oriented vertically, with no bands. Stitching is split Sumac over a grass foundation, with a dyed black Juncus pattern. One motif is quite different from the other four; i.e. a *pattern anomaly* which is a not-uncommon Juaneño trait.

## RMM A1-58 Luiseño Shallow Bowl

In previous discussions it was stated that Luiseño baskets frequently contain two black Juncus bands. The subject bowl has the requisite two bands that enclose a series of connected concentric diamonds. It has a *knot* "start" using Sumac over Yucca fibers. Split Sumac is the stitching material over a foundation of clockwise coiling Deer Grass. Although the rim is severely damaged, its terminal with 8 back stitches is intact

On first observation, the pattern looks rather busy, almost Cahuilla-like, probably due to the numerous (15) diamonds. Rarely does a Luiseño basket contain this many motifs. It was originally identified as Luiseño by the collector and concurred in by 5 individual basketry authorities. (Cain et. al. circa 1980). The basket was collected circa 1900 by Cornelius Rumsey and was well used before that date.

RMM A1-58 Luiseño Shallow Basin
pictured on Figure 16, page 17, *Rods, Bundles, and Stitches*

RMM A1-59 Luiseño Winnowing Tray
as seen on Figure 116, page 62, *Rods, Bundles, and Stitches*

## RMM A1-59 Luiseño Winnowing Tray

Winnowing trays were used by Indian ladies to remove chaff, small pebbles, and grit, from seeds, prior to grinding or cooking. Winnowing trays were subjected to considerable wear and tear. Such is the case here.

This basket is believed to be circa 1900, and is composed primarily of split Sumac over a Deer Grass foundation. Its "start" is of the *knot* type using Sumac over Yucca fibers. The pattern is rather atypical for Luiseños and was referred to as lightning on museum records. It might more logically be called stair steps. Sparse use of a Juncus pattern is a common Luiseño trait. It is interesting to note that the pattern motifs are concentrated near the outer rim.

RMM A1-60 Luiseño Style Bowl
as illustrated on Figure 74, page 67, *Native American Basketry
of Southern California*

## RMM A1-60 Luiseño Style Basin

This interesting bowl is 15 inches in diameter and 5+ inches tall. Its interest lies in the fact that the 9 concentric negative and positive diamonds, enclosed by two black bands, are blocked by very bold black Juncus, a trait not overly common among Luiseño baskets. Two black bands are common, and enclosing design motifs with black bands is common, but blocking out the motifs in such bold black Juncus is not.

Split Sumac was used over a foundation of clockwise coiling Deer Grass. A *pierced wad* type "start" was used with Sumac over Deer Grass tips. Dyed black Juncus makes up the pattern materials. A rather unique feature regarding this basin are the two *pattern anomalies*. There are nine regular blocked negative diamonds, plus two other motifs that are entirely unrelated in shape. Meaning of this anomaly is unknown.

## RMM A1- 63 Luiseño-? Cahuilla Basin

Museum records indicate this 16 inch diameter basin as being *Cahuilla (?)/ Luiseño (?)* and perhaps from Soboba. It was collected circa 1890 by Cornelius Rumsey who, unfortunately, was not overly careful about provenance. The collection date is important because 1890 is very early in the basket renaissance.

Use of blocked, negative, inverted "V's" (*deer hooves)* was common for Cahuilla but not necessarily so for Luiseño weavers. The possible Cahuilla designation probably arises from the number of such pattern blocks (16), each spirally up and to the right. Four is a rather common number in Luiseño baskets. It has a *pierced wad* "start" of Sumac over grass tips. As in previous baskets, split Sumac was wrapped about a clockwise foundation of Deer Grass. There are 10 back stitches on the terminal.

RMM A1-63 Luiseño(?)/Cahuilla (?) Shallow Bowl
See Fig. 121, page 64, *Rods, Bundles, and Stitches*

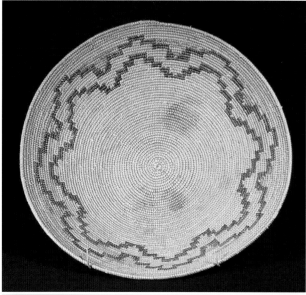

## RMM A1-65 Very Large Shallow Basin

Most Luiseño baskets are either pleasant to gaze upon or are fine works of art. This bowl is neither. It is 18+ inches in diameter, 2+ inches deep and, like many Luiseño baskets, is composed primarily of split Sumac over a clockwise coiling foundation of Deer Grass. Its "start" is of the *bent finger* style of Sumac over grass tips and its terminal is gradual with 12 back stitches.

Unlike many Luiseño baskets, the pattern tends to be rather jumbled, or nervous. This is perhaps due to the fact that the concentric, joined "V's" are more stair stepped than continuous lines. Unfortunately, in a basket with a curved surface and concentric patterns, it is very difficult to keep lines parallel, yet retrain a smooth pattern flow. Based upon the stains on this basket, it was probably used as a household utility piece. Mr. Rumsey collected it circa 1900.

RMM A1-65 Luiseño Shallow Basin
as it appears in Figure 17, page 17, *Rods, Bundles, and Stitches*

## RMM A1-67 Northern Luiseño Winnowing Tray

Winnowing trays were used to separate seed from chaff. Seeds were placed in a flat basket and tossed into the air, allowing wind to blow away everything except seeds. Trays of this style were also used by ladies to roll dice onto, in which case they are known as *gambling trays*. In either case, the tray must be large enough for both the seeds, and dice players, not to be *blown away*. This 18 inches by 2.75 inches tray is about the proper size.

Nineteen joined diamonds are enclosed at their top and bottom. Normally Luiseño patterns are not quite this "busy"; i.e. not quite as many diamonds, but then *"one can never have too many diamonds!"* Dyed black Juncus was used to create the bands and diamonds, while basal red Juncus was used for infilling. Because this basal red Juncus coloration is so weak, the weaver accentuated it with black Juncus.

RMM A1-67 Northern Luiseño Winnowing Tray
see Figure 332, page 177, *Rods, Bundles, and Stitches*

## RMM A1-68 Luiseño Small Burden Basket

Elsewhere in this treatise, there is presented a discussion regarding burden versus storage baskets, both of which are fairly large vessels for gathering or storing food stuffs, and other stuffs. On some occasions, a basket was constructed in much the same shape as a burden basket except being smaller. Such is the case here. Because it was collected circa 1900 and shows evidence of heavy use it was probably intended as a small storage vessel that could also be used for gathering *stuff*. It is almost 13 inches in diameter at the rim, has a flat bottom, with a short terminal but relatively few back stitches. A pierced wad of Deer Grass tips was used for the "start", after which Sumac over grass constitutes the body of the basket. Its pattern is composed of dyed black Juncus. The up-down horizontal pattern actually functions much like horizontal bands.

RMM A1-68 Luiseño Small
Burden Basket
Please see Figure 19 page 18,
*Rods, Bundles, and stitches*

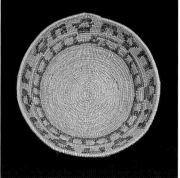

RMM A1-78 Luiseño
Open Basin
*See Figure* 24 page 20,
*Rods, Bundles, and
Stitches*

## RMM A1-78 Luiseño Open Basin

This particular specimen which Cornelius Rumsey collected circa 1910 is not one that many collectors would search out. It is interesting, however, in that it was either a beginner's basket, as indicated in Moser's *Rods, Bundles, and Stitches,* or one created by a weaver in her autumn years. A close look at the pattern motifs suggests that the weaver had extensive experience creating patterns, and was making a very serious effort to tell a story. The fact that the motifs seem to be rather confusing to a 21st century observer does not distract from the mental effort exerted by the weaver.

There is a basal black band, so common on Luiseño baskets, plus extensive use of split Sumac as a background material. Its "start" is of the *knot* style with Sumac over a mix of grass tips and Yucca fibers. The foundation is of Deer Grass and scrap Juncus. No attempt should be made to interpret this pattern.

## RMM A1-79 Luiseño Globular Bowl

The vast majority of "Mission" baskets have a foundation of Deer Grass over which is wrapped either Sumac or Juncus. Occasionally a weaver incorporated scrap Juncus with the Deer Grass. Only rarely is one found with a foundation of shreds of scrap Juncus only. Such is the case with this particular bowl

Although this bowl has a slightly atypical shape, it exhibits most of the traits common to other Luiseño baskets. It begins with a *pierced wad* type of "start" using Sumac over scrap Juncus pieces. It's primary stitching material is split Sumac with dyed black Juncus as a pattern material. There are two black bands with a simple geometric motifs ("running, or joined Vees"). Unlike many Luiseño bowls, this has a rather constricted mouth. which is suggestive of shapes often found in baskets made at Soboba. It was collected by Cornelius Rumsey prior to 1900 and shows some degree of wear.

RMM A1-79 Luiseño Globular Bowl
see Figure 29, page 23, *Rods, Bundles, and Stitches*

RMM A1-82 Luiseño
Storage Basket
as shown in Figure 299,
page150, *Rods,
Bundles, and Stitches*

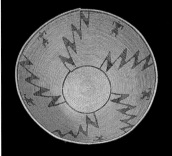

## RMM A1-82 Luiseño Storage/ Burden Basket

To some basketry students, the term *burden basket* conjures up a mental picture of a large cone-shaped basket carried in a net over a lady's back. In Southern California, burden baskets have a flat bottom with only slightly out-flaring sides. They were carried in a mesh carrying net on the lady's back, supported by a "tump line" across her forehead (see photo page 92). As the name implies, they were used to carry almost anything. This particular basket, because its sides flare out quite widely, is probably a storage, not a burden basket. It was collected circa 1900 and undoubtedly was made to be used because baskets for sale were rarely this large. Sumac was used in a *pierced wad* "start" of Deer Grass tips. It is very well ornamented with five *lightning* motifs plus two black bands. Unlike most Luiseño patterns, there are five anthropomorphs (stylized humans). Also unlike most Luiseño baskets, yellow dye was used sparingly in the small flat bottom.

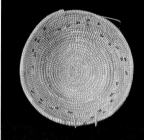

RMM A1-86 Possible
Luiseño Cup
as pictured in Figure 100,
page 69, *Native American
Basketry of Southern
California*

## RMM A1-86 Possible Luiseño Cup

Prior to European contact (1769), Southern California Indians used small baskets quite extensively for dishes, cups, household utensils, and even hats. When well used, such baskets show evidence of oils and food remnants. It is believed this basket was made for sale or as an eating cup but was unused.

Unlike many Luiseño baskets, Juncus is the primary stitching material over a clockwise coiling foundation of Deer Grass. The "start" is of the *pierced wad* style using natural Juncus over a Grass-Juncus mix foundation. The Juncus has a slight greenish cast which suggests it was not thoroughly cured prior to weaving. When first harvested, Juncus is a deep forest green, which is bleached to a tan in the sun often for several months. The fact that it was not well cured suggests it was made by an inexperienced weaver. Black and maroon dyed Juncus dots create a rather austere pattern, again suggesting it was made by a "beginner". It is dated circa 1900.

## RMM A1-87 Luiseño Leaching Tray

One of the most common foods used by nearly all Indians of the western US is a meal made from powdered acorns. Unfortunately acorns are rich in tannin, a bitter, poisonous substance which was removed by first pounding acorns in a mortar or *metate* (stone mortar). To leach out this tannin, pounded acorn meal was placed in an open weave basketry tray which allowed water to pass through but retains the meal. Water was repeatedly poured over the meal, dissolving the tannin, which was flushed away leaving a very tasty dough-like meal.

Leaching trays have a foundation of coarse material which results in an open sieve-like porosity. This particular tray has an *overhand knot* "start" of Sumac over scrap Juncus. Shredded scrap Juncus makes up its foundation. It was collected circa 1900 and could be either Luiseño, Cahuilla or even Diegueño.

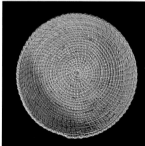

RMM A1-87 Luiseño
Leaching Tray
Please see Figure 126, page
66, *Rods, Bundles, and
Stitches*

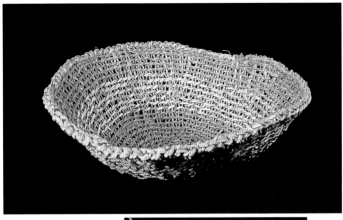

## RMM A1-88 Luiseño Leaching Tray

To some basket collectors, whole Juncus twined baskets are classified as *"Throw-Away"* because they were made very quickly and then generally discarded after one or several uses. (Early Indian homes did not have an over abundance of storage space for seldom used items.) To some collectors, they are *"Open weave twined leaching trays"*.

Tannin is both a bitter and poisonous component of acorn meal, so, as the name implies, leaching trays were used to remove that tannin from acorn flour. Leaves or grasses often lined the basket, upon which acorn flour was placed and perhaps a dozen flushings of water was applied to leach out the bitterness.

Open weave twining, as in this tray, is the only example of basketry twining in Southern California.

RMM A1-88 Luiseño
Leaching Tray
see figure 196, page
105, *Rods, Bundles,
and Stitches*

## RMM A1-89 Wide Luiseño Basin

Cornelius Rumsey collected this large basket prior to 1900 so it represent a style and pattern in use prior to the *basket renaissance* starting in the early 1900's. After 1900, outside influences often dictated basketry shapes, styles, and patterns. Note that this design is simple but pleasing which presumably reflects designs of the late 1800's. Note also the extensive wear on the rim, which means it may have been old in the 1890's.

The "start" is very crude and may be an old Indian repair, which would further add to the antiquity of this basket. As might be expected, Sumac over Deer Grass is the primary stitching material. Because of rim damage, little can be said of the terminal.

RMM A1-89 Wide Luiseño
Basin
see Figure 79, page 67,
*Native American Basketry of
Southern California*

## RMM A1-92 Luiseño Storage Basket

It is the author's opinion that most collectors refer to almost any very large Indian basket as a *"Burden basket"*, whereas many of them were probably created for storage. A burden basket tends to have more vertical sides than does a storage basket. This specific basket is perhaps wider than a burden basket should be. ERGO, it is referred to herein as a storage basket.

Its "start" is a *Pierced Wad* using Sumac over Deer Grass tips, while the basic stitching material is split Sumac over a foundation of whole Deer Grass. Dyed black and basal red Juncus was used for the pattern motifs. Unlike many Luiseño baskets, this one has a single band of alternating black Juncus and Sumac one coil in from the rim.

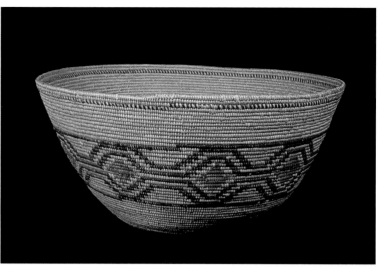

RMM A1-92 Luiseño Storage Basket
as seen in Figure 246, page 128, *Rods, Bundles, and Stitches*

RMM A1-94 Luiseño
Storage Basket
see Figure 57, page 65,
*Native American Basketry
of Southern California*

## RMM A1-94 Luiseño Storage Basket

Virtually everything said about basket A1-92 above is applicable to this storage basket. Its rim is even larger than A1-92 and its height about the same. Both were collected circa 1900 and this basket shows considerable wear about the rim, which suggests that it saw extensive use during the 1890's, or earlier. Because of its probable dating, it would seem that the maker did not intend this one be placed on the Non-Indian market.

The weaver used a *Pierced Wad* type of "start" using Sumac over grass tips. Juncus was then used over a foundation of Deer Grass seed stalks. Unlike many such baskets, the weaver placed an irregular pattern anomaly in the connected diamond on the very left edge of the banded pattern.

## RMM A1-95 Large Luiseño Basin

During the period 1890 to 1910, Cornelius Rumsey collected Indian baskets extensively throughout southern California. Many which he acquired were of the utility type. This is just such a basket; i.e. approximately 24+ inches in diameter at the rim and estimated to be circa 1890 or earlier. Unlike many Luiseño baskets, this was made almost entirely of Juncus over a Deer Grass foundation. The weaver used a *Knot* "start" of Juncus over Yucca fibers, which is quite common for most "Mission" baskets but not common for Luiseño baskets. Its austere pattern is simply two black Juncus bands.

RMM A1-95 Large Luiseño Basin
as seen in Figure 63, page 65, *Native American Basketry of Southern California*

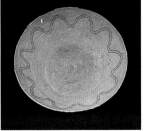

RMM A1-96 Large Luiseño Basin
please see Figure 6, page 12, *Rods, Bundles, and Stitches*

## RMM A1-96 Large Luiseño Basin

RMM is very fortunate to have acquired a large number of Indian baskets which were collected by Cornelius E. Rumsey prior to 1900, and thus represent styles reflecting an *endangered culture*. The subject utility basin was undoubtedly created for utility or household use, as evidenced by extensive rim and side damage. RMM records indicate this to be "possible *Serrano*", which the author does not believe to be the case. Its "start" is of the *Pierced Wad* style with Sumac over grass tips. Except for the rather austere pattern of connected half domes of black Juncus, the entire basket is of Sumac weaver strands over a foundation of Deer Grass seed stalks. Many Serrano baskets contain a more colorful and showy pattern, using more basal red Juncus.

RMM A1-97 Luiseño Burden Basket
see Figure 333, page 177, *Rods, Bundles, and Stitches*

## RMM A1-97 Luiseño Burden Basket

Narrative accompanying baskets A1-92 and A1-94 addresses burden versus storage baskets, both of which are considered herein to be storage baskets. The subject basket, A1-97, is what the author believes should more properly be called a Burden Basket. Its rim is almost 22 inches in diameter and the sides are more nearly vertical than on a storage basket.

A *Bent Finger* "start" was used with Sumac over Deer Grass tips. The remainder is also Sumac over a grass foundation. Note the two styles of motifs, one a horizontal series of "flat mountains" and the other spiraling rectangles.

## RMM A1-99 Luiseño Deep Tray

Large basketry trays were used for a variety of purposes, not the least of which is for winnowing seeds and grains. They also served as storage vessels, laundry baskets, and for cooking. This 17+ inches, 1890–1900 tray is of split Sumac over a foundation of Deer Grass. The pattern is of dyed black Juncus and there are old repairs. Although it does not have the usual black bands, the pattern is horizontal in orientation with four motifs that are slightly suggestive of *cogs* or *"dogs"* on the wheel of a turn-of-the-century piece of farm machinery.

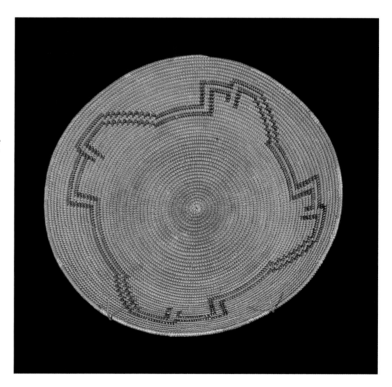

RMM A1-99 Large Luiseño Tray
as shown on Figure 14, page 16, *Rods Bundles, and Stitches*

RMM A1-138 Small Luiseño Bowl
see also Figure 23 page 20, *Rods, Bundles, and Stitches*

## RMM A1-138 Small Luiseño Bowl

It has been said that not all Indian baskets are works of art. That is certainly true of this particular basket. It was created either by a beginner or a lady in her autumn years, based not only upon its crude workmanship, but also on her choice and use of materials. Split Sumac is the basic stitching material but the weaver was careless trimming it to a uniform width and was even more careless by splitting stitches on both the work and non-work side. She used a *Bent Finger* "start" with a mixture of foundation materials, primarily whole Juncus, split Juncus, and Deer Grass. Stitches are widely spaced, thus exposing foundation materials to view. This is very common for beginning weavers. It was collected circa 1910 by Cornelius Rumsey.

## RMM A8-120 Luiseño Deep Basin

This is the first basket in this catalogue collected by Harwood Hall, a former superintendent of the Sherman Institute (Indian school) in Riverside, California. It is dated circa 1900. Mr. Hall collected numerous baskets and other Indian items throughout Southern California. Most of his collection is addressed later in Chapter 9. Museum records attribute this one to a Luiseño weaver but this author believes the weaver may have been born as, or related to, the Juaneño people near San Juan Capistrano. That supposition is based upon the vertical orientation of rather isolated pattern motifs. The weaver used a *Knot* "start" of Sumac over Yucca fiber, with the body of Sumac over Deer Grass. The pattern is of black Juncus and there are no horizontal bands nor is there a horizontal orientation to the pattern, so common in Luiseño baskets. Its rim is approximately 14+ inches in diameter.

RMM A8-120 Luiseño Deep Basin
as shown in Figure 243 page 126, *Rods, Bundles, and Stitches*

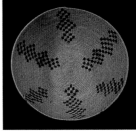

**RMM A8-129 Luiseño Globular Gift Bowl**

Although there is no standard shape for a gift bowl, this basket is rather typical for such baskets made by Cahuilla, Serrano, Luiseño, and Diegueño weavers. It is almost 6 inches wide at the base and *bellies out* about midway up the side, with its base and rim approximately equal in diameter. Its *Pierced Wad* type "start" is of Sumac over grass tips. Sumac is the stitching material over a foundation of Deer Grass. Dyed black and pale basal red Juncus was used to create the pattern. Diamonds are in pairs with sides truncated, while the tops and bottoms are pointed. Diamond are also infilled with pale red Juncus. Harwood Hall collected this bowl c. 1900.

RMM A8-129 Luiseño Gift Bowl
please see Figure 186 page102, *Rods, Bundles, and Stitches*

RMM A11-2 Luiseño Small
Burden Basket
as pictured in Figure 184 page
102 *Rods, Bundles, and Stitches*

**RMM A11-2 Small Burden Basket**

Museum records list this as a burden basket but its shape is atypical; i.e. the sides are more vertical and its bottom is more convex than are other such burden baskets. Unlike many Luiseño baskets, this one has a *Knot* "start" of Sumac over Yucca fibers. The primary stitching material is Sumac over Deer Grass. It has the ubiquitous two black bands but the top band is almost at the rim and the bottom is indeed at the bottom. The six sets of lightning-like motifs are typical from Southern California and wind up and to the left. This basket is circa 1900–1910.

Attention is directed to basket RMM A1-82, page 34. Its bands are also near the rim and at the very base but its lightning bolts wind up and to the right, as viewed from the inside.

## RMM A31-5 Luiseño Burden Basket

It was stated previously that burden basket sides do not normally flare out as they do on storage baskets. This basket's sides flare only slightly in comparison to a storage basket. Its "start" is the *Bent Finger* style with Sumac over grass tips. Primary stitching material is split Sumac over a Deer Grass foundation. Dyed black Juncus was used to create a horizontal pattern which somewhat resembles a net design, sans a top and bottom band. This basket was presented to State Senator H.M. Streeter by an Indian lady circa 1890. Indians are (were) *incorrigible givers* and it was not uncommon for Indian people to give baskets to friends, or persons of importance, albeit not such big ones.

RMM A31-5 Luiseño Burden Basket
as shown in Figure 12 page 14, *Rods, Bundles, and Stitches*

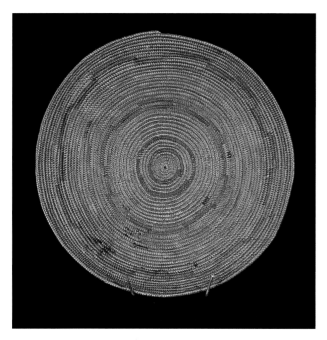

RMM A83-262 Luiseño Tray
Please see Figure 218 page 118, *Rods, Bundles, and Stitches*

## RMM A83-262 Luiseño Tray

Museum records refer to this simply as a *tray*. It might be suggested that the word *parching* could be added. A parching tray is one in which seeds were placed covering the basketry bottom. A red hot live coal(s) was then added and the entire mass was swirled so as not to burn the basket but to toast (parch) the seeds. In spite of the skill of an Indian lady, the basket occasionally became scorched, as has this one.

It is not unduly large for a working tray, being only 13 inches in diameter. Split Sumac is the stitching material over a foundation of Deer Grass. Dyed black Juncus was used to create the rather austere pattern, which consists of several circular single black bands in the base, plus two *up-down* linear black bands (*"low flat mountains"*) near the top. The basket is circa 1890 or possibly earlier.

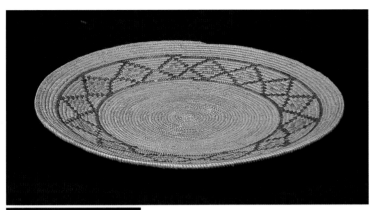

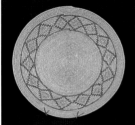

Rmm A83-263 Luiseño Tray
as shown in Figure 119 page 71,
*Native American Basketry of
Southern California*

## RMM A83-263 Luiseño Winnowing Tray

It is suggested that the reader review basket RMM A1-67, page 32, to note similarities with this basket. Both are winnowing trays, this one being 15 inches in diameter, slightly less than RMM A1-67. This one also has fewer diamonds in the pattern. However, the two are otherwise very similar and could, conceivably, have been made by the same weaver. Both have a *Pierced Wad* "start" of Sumac over Grass tips. Split Sumac was used to wrap a foundation of Deer Grass. Dyed black Juncus outlines the enclosed 14 diamonds, which have a natural but pale basal red Juncus center. The basket is dated simply *"early 20th century"*.

## RMM A83-277 Luiseño Tray

Not all basketry trays were used for winnowing or parching. This 14 inch tray, although being made during the late 1800's, was probably intended for light household utility purposes. That supposition is based upon the fact that Juncus, not Sumac, was used to create the bulk of its side. Juncus is a reed and is quite easy to split and prepare for weaving, as compared with Sumac. On the other hand, Sumac is a much tougher, more durable material and is used whenever rough use is anticipated. Juncus is often used in a utility basket only when a color pattern is desired. In this particular case the tougher Sumac was used on the base and rim rather than the weaker Juncus. However, the sides are of Juncus, suggesting its use would be less intense.

RMM A83-277 Luiseño
Tray
see Figure 312 page 156,
*Rods, Bundles, and Stitches*

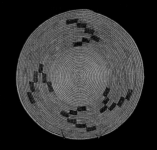

RMM A83-297 Luiseño Burden Basket
as pictured in Figure 10, page 13, *Rods, Bundles, and Stitches*

### RMM A83-297 Luiseño Burden Basket

Although this large basket has the two black bands, so typical of Luiseño baskets, the isolated black crosses enclosed by the bands are suggestive of a Juaneño basket. Luiseño weavers occasionally placed isolated pattern motifs within the two black bands. However, such motifs are rarely scattered as in this example. Orientation of the crosses suggests that they were very subtly arranged in an *Up-down, running vee* pattern, which is not uncommon on Luiseño baskets.

The basket has an 18 inch rim diameter but its width-vs-height suggests it was made primarily for storage. Wear on the rim and inside indicates it was used for many moons before being collected by Mr. and Mrs S. Leonard Herrick in the late 1890's. Like many Luiseño baskets, it has a *Pierced Wad* "start" of Sumac around Deer Grass tips. Sumac was also used as a wrapping material over grass seed stalks for its foundation. The black bands and pattern motifs are of dyed black Juncus with no basal red Juncus visible.

### RMM A116-1 Luiseño Burden Basket

Like the preceding basket, this is a very typical Southern California utility basket which is often called a burden basket but more properly might be called a storage vessel. It has been classified as being Luiseño primarily on the basis of its two horizontal back Juncus bands enclosing a simple double set of connected "V's". Although that style of pattern is typical of Luiseño baskets in general, many "Mission Indian" weavers used a similar pattern on their burden/storage basket. Rarely did Southern California weavers place a complex pattern motif on a storage basket unless it was made for sale to a Non-Indian collector.

This basket was collected by William Collier in 1890, very early in the basket renaissance (1900–1930), which means it presumably was made to be used, not for sale. Note, however, the simple but pleasing pattern on a utility basket intended for heavy use.

RMM A116-1 Luiseño Burden Basket
photographed as Figure 20, page 18, *Rods, Bundles, and Stitches*

## RMM A144-8 Luiseño Flared Basin

Interestingly enough, this basket has a number of characteristics attributable to the Juaneño people; i.e. seven vertically oriented geometric motifs rotating horizontally about the basket's sides, with no bands or other pattern elements. Although such pattern orientation suggests Juaneño, there is an aura about this specific basket which virtually screams that it is Luiseño, not Juaneño.

Like many Luiseño baskets, a *Pierced Wad* "start" of Sumac over Deer Grass tips was used. The remainder of the basket is split Sumac over a clockwise coiling foundation of Deer Grass, with dyed black Juncus for pattern materials. Accession records indicate it was collected by *"Mrs. Hall's Father"* circa 1900–1920. Mrs. Halls Father was actually Mr. Chauncey L. McFarland. Stains on the bottom suggest it was well used by its previous owner prior to arrival of *Mrs. Hall's father.* The flared sides is rather typical for a working basket and further confirms it as a utility basket.

RMM A144-8 Luiseño Flared Basin
depicted as Figure 362, page 188, *Rods, Bundles, and Stitches,* and page 67, *Native American Basketry of Southern California*

RMM A144-11 Luiseño Burden Basket
Full page photo on page 15, *Rod, Bundles, and Stitches.*

## RMM A144-11 Burden Basket

Attention is drawn to the various burden baskets previously pictured herein; viz. A1-92, A31-5, and A116-1. All are relatively short with respect to their width, implying they were probably made for storage with a secondary use as a gathering vessel. This one is not overly large; i.e. approximately 16 inches in diameter at the top but has a relatively small base. It has the ubiquitous two black bands enclosing a series of connected stacked diamonds, which is rather common on Luiseño burden baskets. It also has a shape that flares out only slightly as it rises but retains a flat base. The weaver used a *Knot* type "start" with Sumac over grass seed stalk tips, then continued with Sumac over a Deer Grass foundation. An interesting feature is that the work side (the nicer looking surface) is on the INSIDE. One would expect the nicer side to face outward. However, when the basket is empty, it probably sat on the floor so a viewer looked DOWN into it and admired the inside, not the outside.

## RMM A313-13 Large Luiseño Bowl/Basin

This fairly large basin is listed as possibly being of Juaneño origin. However, there is a question in the author's mind as to that possibility. The blocked-in negative triangles could be Juaneño only if they were not so numerous and did not spiral outward, which is more commonly thought of as being a Serrano or Cahuilla trait. Being nearly 14 inches in diameter, it is larger than many such basins.

The "start" is of the *Knot* style using Sumac over split Juncus and grass tips. Sumac was then used over a foundation of Deer Grass for the bulk of the basket, with dyed black Juncus forming the pattern. The stair steps swirls up and to the left, when viewed from the basket's inside. A cursory study of spiral direction does not seem to point to any consistency, either by Luiseños, Serranos, or Cahuillas. This basket was collected circa 1900 and does not show any appreciable wear, which may mean it was made for sale.

RMM A313-13 Luiseño Open Bowl
see Figure 77, page 67, *Native American Basketry of Southern California,* also Figure 366, page 189, *Rods, Bundles, and Stitches*

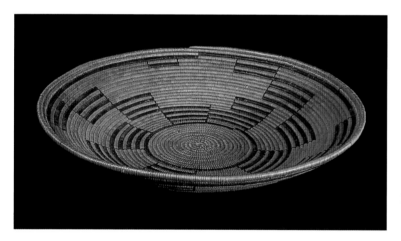

RMM A319-1(2) Luiseño Tray
It is pictured as Figure 322, page 160, *Rods, Bundles, and Stitches*

## RMM A319-1(2) Northern Luiseño Tray

Museum records indicate this circa 1910 basket to be possibly of Cahuilla origin. It has a rather *busy* pattern, as do many Cahuilla baskets, and makes extensive use of natural buff Juncus on its body, rather than Sumac. The pattern, however, is more geometric than are many Cahuilla baskets, which suggests possibly Luiseño influence. Although most of the baskets in this exhibit contain Sumac almost exclusively as a stitching material, this basket has Sumac only on the very bottom. The "start" is of the *Bent Finger* type with Sumac over Juncus pieces. Its primary foundation is of Deer Grass with black dyed Juncus making up the pattern.

The 3 and 4 bar stair step design is not at all common on Luiseño baskets but it has two black bands enclosing the pattern, one on top and one near the bottom. Attention is drawn to the pattern anomaly which resembles an aborted stair step at 12:00 o'clock in the photo. Workmanship is too exact for this to be accidental.

RMM A319-1(3) Luiseño Winnowing Tray
see photograph in Figure 111, page 70, *Native American Baskets of Southern California*

### RMM A319-1(3) Luiseño Winnowing Tray

Rarely does one have the opportunity to see a Southern California basket older than circa 1880. This 18 inch diameter tray is *believed* to be from the middle 19th century (1850). It has a *Pierced Wad* "start" of Juncus over pieces of Juncus. Split natural buff colored Juncus was used as a wrapping material over a foundation of Deer Grass that coils clockwise. The two bands are of dyed black Juncus with no other pattern.

A word about Juncus versus Sumac . . . As for ease in weaving, Juncus is by far the easiest and fastest. Splitting longitudinally and trimming for width is easy and done quickly. Sumac, on the other hand, takes perhaps 5 times as long to prepare, however, it is far superior to Juncus for durability whenever heavy wear was anticipated. The fact that Sumac was not used on this utility tray suggests that Sumac may not have been readily available.

### RMM A955-2 Luiseño Storage Basket

This is an exceptionally fine 18 inch diameter storage basket which is listed on museum records as a burden basket. *(burden baskets may serve as storage baskets, but storage baskets are not necessarily burden baskets).* As for its shape, it is rather typical for a Southern California basket. It has the two horizontal black bands which enclose a pattern of horizontally joined geometric motifs. Orientation of the motifs is somewhat atypical for a "Mission Basket". There are horizontally arranged sets of 3 to 5 upward pointing teeth-like triangles, joined by another set pointing down. Ironically, the number of *teeth* per set varies, with more teeth pointing down than pointing up.

The basket has a *Pierced Wad* " "start"of Sumac over grass tips. The remainder has split Sumac wrapped about a clockwise coiling foundation of Deer Grass. Dyed black Juncus was used to create the two single black bands, as well as the pattern motifs. It was collected circa 1900 and is in excellent condition, suggesting little wear.

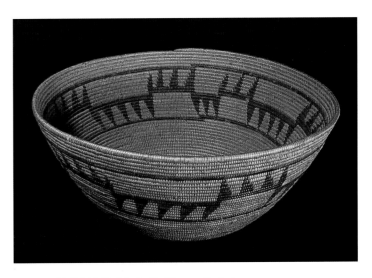

RMM A955-2 Luiseño Storage Basket
as seen in Figure 369, page 190, *Rods, Bundles, and Stitches*

47

RMM A1236-11 Luiseño Bowl
as seen in Figure 106, page 70, *Native American Basketry of Southern California*

## RMM A1236-11 Luiseño Globular Bowl

Of the generic Luiseño baskets described in this narrative, only 4 are globular bowls, the rest being either flattish trays, burden or storage baskets, or large open basins. During the basket renaissance (1900–1930), use of large working baskets declined dramatically due to the availability of metal pots and pans. Most baskets of this era were made for sale, many being small gift or globular type because they were easier to make and sold more readily. This is not to say that pre-1900 globular bowls did not exist. It merely says that 1900–1930 baskets are more apt to be globular or small gift types with pre-1900 baskets inclining toward the more utilitarian types.

This late 1890's, 9 inch diameter bowl has a *Bent Finger* "start" of Juncus over grass tips. The remainder is of natural and dyed Juncus on a clockwise Deer Grass foundation. It was probably made as a *Treasure* basket.

## RMM A1236-18 Luiseño Globular Bowl

Please note the similarity between this and the previous bowl, RMM 1236-11. There is little question in the mind of the author that the two were made by the same weaver. Although this one is 1/4" larger at the shoulder, it is about 3/4" shorter than the previous basket. They were both collected c. 1900 by Mr. and Mrs. Frank Miller, of *MISSION INN* fame, where the baskets resided for many years

The primary pattern motif strongly resembles that on the previous basket, albeit not quite like a stylized plant, or if so, a plant not yet in bloom. There are 3 such motifs here whereas only 2 on the previous bowl. Natural and dyed black Juncus are the stitching and pattern material over a foundation of clockwise coiling Deer Grass.

RMM A1236-18 Luiseño Globular Bowl
as pictured in Figure 107, page 70, *Native American Basketry of Southern California*

## RMM A1236-36 Luiseño Burden Basket

Luiseño burden baskets seem to have a shape very much in common with that of most other Southern California Indian tribes. This specimen, which is presumed to be a burden, not a storage basket, is no exception. It is almost 22 inches in diameter and 13+ inches tall. It was obtained by Mr. and Mrs Frank Miller circa 1900 and was displayed at the *Mission Inn* for many years. It has a *Bent Finger* "start" of Sumac over grass tips. The main body is composed of split Sumac over a grass foundation. Pattern elements are of dyed black Juncus. Its pattern contains two single black bands of black Juncus enclosing 3 concentric sets of joined "Vees". "Vees" were frequently used and joined within the two black bands. This specific pattern is somewhat unique in that the trough between the inverted "Vees" widens at the top due to the pattern being concentric and expanding. The weaver handled this very well.

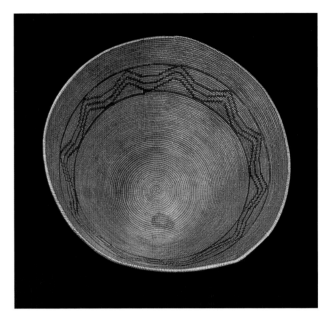

RMM A1236-36 Luiseño Burden Basket
please see Figure 55, page 65, *Native American Basketry of Southern California*

RMM A1236-37 Luiseño Storage Basket
as seen in Figure 62, page 65, *Native American basketry of Southern California*

## RMM A1236-37 Luiseño Storage Basket

In previous descriptions, the difference between a burden and a storage basket has been noted. This specific basket is exemplary. It is quite wide at the rim but not unduly tall. Had it been a burden (gathering) basket the lady could not have accommodated the wide rim while carrying it in an over-the-back net (see photo page 92). A greater depth but narrower rim would be more to her advantage. ERGO, the basket was presumably made to store *things*, not to gather them.

This basket was collected c.1900 by the Frank Millers and resided many years at their Mission Inn. It has the requisite two black bands enclosing black joined diamonds with basal red Juncus infilling. The field is Sumac over Deer Grass seed stalks.

49

**RMM A1236-39 Luiseño Storage Basket**

This 16 inch diameter, 7 inch tall storage/burden basket was collected by Frank Miller, prior to 1905 and was displayed in the Mission Inn's tea room before that room was demolished in 1905. The Millers, for decades, operated the famous Mission Inn (hotel) which is located diagonally across the intersection from the current Riverside Municipal Museum. That hotel is still in operation, although it has been remodeled several times since 1905.

This basket is one of only a relatively few Luiseño burden or storage baskets made exclusively of natural and colored Juncus. Although it has a single black Juncus band at the very top and one at the base, the bands do not serve as pattern elements; i.e. the top band is too small and serves almost as a colored rim. The three vertical stacked triangle *"tree"* motifs, sans the black bands, are often associated with Cahuilla baskets. Therefore, this basket may have strong Cahuilla ties.

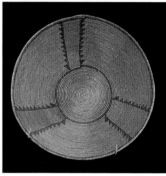

RMM A1236-39 Luiseño Storage Basket as shown in Figure 65, page 66, *Native American Basketry of Southern California*

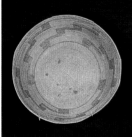

RMM A1236-40 Luiseño Storage Basket also seen as Figure 69, page 66, *Native American Basketry of Southern California*

**RMM A1236-40 Luiseño Storage Basket**

It was stated on a previous page that storage bowls may be as large, or even larger at the rim than a burden basket but generally not as tall. This is a good example. This one is 17.5 inches in diameter and 6.5 inches tall. Note that the sides of this basket flare out more than do those on the above basket. Like the previous basket, this one is composed of natural split Juncus stitching over a foundation of Deer Grass. Its "start" is of the *Pierced Wad* style of Juncus over grass tips. Pattern material is entirely of dyed black Juncus with no natural basal red coloration. It contains a rather innocuous black horizontal band at the top of the five spirals of up-and-to-the-right stair steps.

The Frank Millers collected this basket circa 1900 and displayed it at the Mission Inn for many years.

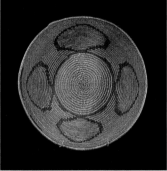

RMM A1236-45 Luiseño
Large Basin
*see Figure 80, page 67,
Native American Basketry
of Southern California.*

## RMM A1236-45 Luiseño Storage Bowl (possibly number A83-265)

There appears to be a discrepancy in accession numbers regarding this basket. Although it bears the number A1236-40, records also show it as being A83-265, which signifies a donation by Mr. S. Leonard and Margaret Herrick. It is over 17 inches diameter at the rim and 5+ inches tall, which would place it into the wide basin- short storage basket category, except that its base is quite small in comparison with its mouth. It is almost exclusively of natural Juncus stitching over a foundation of Deer Grass.

Unlike many Luiseño baskets, split Sumac was used as a stitching material only on the top, or outer 4 coils. This is very interesting in that Sumac is acknowledged as being a very durable material and used on the rim whenever wear was anticipated. It would seem, therefore, that its weaver intended this basket to be heavily used.

Please note the two isolated short black stripes near the outer rim. These may have been the weaver's signature.

## RMM 1236-47 Luiseño Basin

This basket is dated middle-late 19th century and was on display at the Mission Inn for many years. Because of its widely flaring sides and small base it is called herein, a basin rather than a storage basket. Its "start" is of the *Bent Finger* style of Juncus over grass tips. Natural Juncus is the primary stitching material over a foundation of Deer Grass.

An interesting treatment was given to the design motifs. The weaver first created 5 sets of three joined diamonds in a triangular orientation. The bottom two in each set have basal red Juncus filling the interior but the upper triangles have Sumac outlining the basal red Juncus center. The weaver then created one motif of only two diamonds, one on top of the other, creating what may be called a pattern anomaly. Inasmuch as this wide basin was collected in the late 19th century, it was presumably not made for the general market. None-the-less, it shows great artistic qualities.

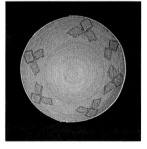

RMM A1236-47 Luiseño Basin
as pictured in Figure 72, page
66, *Native American Basketry of
Southern California*

RMM A1240-3 Deep Luiseño
Basin
as shown as Figure 76, page
67, *Native American Basketry
of Southern California*

### RMM A1240-3 Deep Luiseño Basin

Some years ago the Riverside Unified
School District was given a small collection
of Indian baskets for purposes of teaching
grade school children about California
Indians. Although the school staff used the
baskets for this purpose, the baskets,
themselves, became *well used* and sorely in
need of curation. The collection was
therefore donated to the Riverside Municipal Museum, whose staff placed the items
in a state of *arrested deterioration.* This
particular basket is almost 17 inches in
diameter, is 5 inches tall, and is estimated to
be circa the middle-late 19th century.

Although the basket has two black dyed Juncus
bands enclosing the pattern, it is one of a very few
Luiseño baskets with anthropomorphic (human) and
zoomorphic (animal) pattern motifs; i.e. cowboys
roping horses. It was apparently considered to be
Luiseño based upon the two black Juncus bands.
Otherwise it resembles Cahuilla patterns. Its "start" is
a *Bent Finger* using Sumac over Deer Grass tips. The
primary stitching is Sumac over a grass foundation.

### RMM A1240-6 Luiseño Storage Bowl

This is the second in the baskets from the
Riverside Unified School District. Like
the previous basket, it was used for years
to demonstrate California Indian life to
young children and is suffering from hard
usage and advanced old age ( possibly
middle 19th century). It is almost 18
inches in diameter at the rim and nearly
6 inches in height.

The bottom of this basket is of split
Sumac over a clockwise coiling foundation of Deer Grass, which suggests it was
intended as a utilitarian vessel. The
weaver apparently signed the bottom
using 4 red Juncus stitches. Its sides contains two
horizontal bands of dyed black Juncus, enclosing 4
groups of pattern elements, each with vertical *trees;*
i.e. sets of two vertical columns of basal red Juncus,
containing opposed horizontal triangles attached to
the vertical element. Needless to say, the basket is in
a rather deteriorated condition.

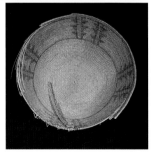

RMM A1240-6 Luiseño Storage
Bowl
please see Fig. 70, p. 66, *Native
American Basketry of Southern
California*

## RMM A1240-7 Large, Deep Luiseño Basin

This is the third of four Luiseño baskets from the Riverside Unified School collection, as discussed above. Although the size is not readily apparent in the photo, this basket is over 24 inches in diameter and nearly 10 inches tall. Like the first two from this collection, it is quite old, perhaps middle 19th century, and in a relatively *"well used"* condition, although not as badly worn as A1240-3, and A1240-6. Being from the middle 19th century, these baskets were undoubtedly made as utility vessels, before easy access to metal pots and pans. Extensive wear seems to bear out this supposition.

The "start" on this one is of the *Pierced Wad* type using Sumac over a fiber foundation. Primary materials are Sumac over a Deer Grass foundation with dyed black Juncus in the pattern. There is no provenance nor are black bands resent. However, the series of concentric horizontally joined diamonds strongly suggest it is of Luiseño origin.

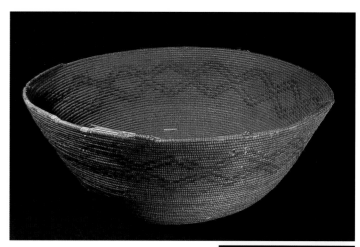

RMM A1240-7 Deep Luiseño Basin
please see Figure 294, page 119, *Native American Basketry of Southern California*

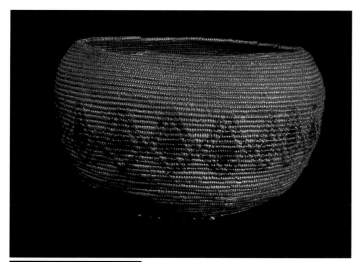

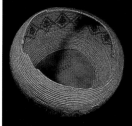

RMM A1240-9 Luiseño Globular Bowl
As shown in Figure 110, page 70, *Native American Basketry of Southern California*

## RMM A1240-9 Luiseño Globular Bowl

Museum records suggest that this may possibly be of Gabrielino origin, perhaps based upon the Deer Grass/split Juncus foundation mix. While split Juncus in a foundation is not exceedingly rare in Luiseño baskets, it was not normally used. Gabrielino baskets, on the other hand, are known for their whole and/or split Juncus foundation, not unlike those of the Chumash.

This 10 inch diameter, 8 inch tall bowl is the only globular shaped Luiseño baskets in this School District series. In spite of the excessive rim damage, the basket faintly resembles the *Degekup* shape of Washoe baskets ( Lake Tahoe). Ironically, *Degekup* shapes were not developed in Washoe baskets until the 1920's. Horizontally oriented band of joined concentric diamonds could be either Luiseño or Gabrielino in style. This basket is estimated to be circa middle 19th century and has a linoleum patch on the bottom, probably by the original owner or early user.

***Esperanza Sobenish, a close-up of her starting a basket***

Mr. Edward Davis captured Mrs. Esperanza Sobenish on film in 1919 on the
Rincon reservation as she began creating a large flat bottom basket. Apparently
Mr. Davis, on the same visit, also took photographs of Mrs. Sobenish working on
a large basket with a rattlesnake design. An original print of this photograph was
given to the author by Mrs. Ann Davis, Ed. Davis' granddaughter.

# CHAPTER 8

# *Soboba Baskets*

### Basket Descriptions

Although the Soboba reservation is technically located well within Cahuilla territory, not in Luiseno country, eight Soboba baskets have been selected for inclusion in this treatise because they exhibit Luiseno traits or have accession records indicating *Soboba/Luiseno* origins. Inasmuch as most Indians living on the Soboba reservation trace their lineage to the Luiseno, Cahuilla, Serrano, Gabrielino, Diegueno, or some combination thereof, baskets found on this reservations often vary widely in shapes and design. Several rather unique shapes evolved from this hybridization; viz. a *pear shape, a stretched neck,* and a *spittoon* style.

The first, or *pear shape*, has a rather squat appearance with its greatest diameter at the "belly" or lower 1/4 of its height. Almost universally, this *Pear shape* is confined to baskets from Soboba. On rare occasions, one will be found that is attributed to a Cahuilla weaver.

The *stretched neck* shape has gently curving sides, similar to a globular bowl, but near the neck, that curing straightens out and may, at an extreme, even become slightly out-curving, giving the impression that someone pulled, or stretched, the neck upward.

The *spittoon* shape vaguely replicates an *olla (clay water vessel)*, with a normal curving belly and shoulder. The neck, however, starts curving inward, then reverses, curving outward to form the semblance of a lip, as on an old fashion spittoon. This shape occurs in globular bowls and is generally found along a corridor starting in the vicinity of Campo-Jacumba in southeastern San Diego County almost at the international border, then extending north-westerly along the west slopes of Mount Laguna, passed Lake Cuyamaca, Julian, Santa Ysabel, Aguanga, Hemet, and ending near Soboba. Quite naturally, the corridor is not chiseled in stone nor is it even a well defined corridor. In fact, this belt is recognized by only a very limited number of basketry students (the author being one). Because some baskets in this corridor, or "belt", exhibit this slight spittoon shape, the corridor is sometimes referred to as the *"spittoon belt.* In most cases, baskets exhibiting a spittoon shape were created by Diegueno weavers. However, those in the northern reach of this "belt" are mostly from Soboba.

Because Soboba baskets are not normally associated with, or attributed to those of the Luisenos, only a limited number are included herein, and those primarily for visualization only.

## RMM A1-29 Soboba Style Bowl

It was stated on the previous page that some bowls, or trinket baskets, from the Soboba reservation tend to have their greatest diameter; i.e. the *belly*, low on the side. This bowl's greatest diameter is approximately 1/4 the way up from the base. It has a dyed black Juncus band at the top and bottom, which is typical of many Luiseño baskets. Luiseño baskets do not normally contain stylized motifs such as the *corn stalks, as* on this basket. This is a design motif often associated with Cahuilla weavers.

Because this basket is slightly oval in plan view, the "start" is an elongated *Bent Finger* type. Sumac over grass tips was used on the base. However, the primary stitching material on its side is buff Juncus, with the pattern of dyed black Juncus. The Rumseys collected this 7 inch tall basket early in the 20th century and it was very likely made for sale.

RMM A1-29 Soboba Style Bowl
as shown in Figure 167, page 92,
*Native American Basketry of Southern California*

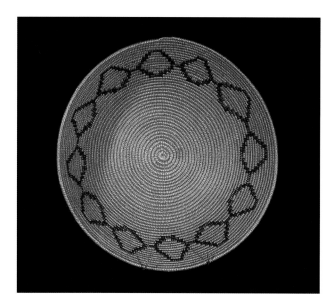

RMM A1-53 Large Luiseño Basin
see Figure 244, page 127,
*Rods, Bundles, and Stitches*

## RMM A1-53 Large Soboba/Luiseno Basin

Museum records indicate this 14.5 inch open basin is *"Luiseño, probably Soboba"*. No supporting information is given as to why it is *". . . probably Soboba"*. In appearance it is typically Luiseño. Its "start" is of the *Bent Finger* style with Sumac over a bundle of Yucca fibers. Stitching material is split Sumac over a Deer Grass foundation and the rather austere pattern of joined diamonds was created of dyed black Juncus.

Cornelius Rumsey collected this basket circa 1900 but gave no indication of its origin or weaver. If, indeed, it is from the Soboba reservation, and there certainly were Luiseño weavers at that reservation in 1900, then this weaver was kept well insulated from influences by Cahuilla, Serrano, Gabrielino, or Diegueño weavers.

## RMM A1-71 Soboba/Luiseño Bowl

A casual glance at workmanship and style on this basket suggests that it was created fairly early in the basket renaissance (circa 1900 to 1930) and made for sale to a tourist. It is 9 inches in diameter, which is quite large for a basket made for sale. Generally, baskets of this style were smaller because a weaver could make a smaller basket faster than a larger one, yet command a similar sale price.

It has the very low center of gravity (fat belly) and the gradual changing curvature which is so common on Soboba baskets. However, its neck is relatively small, in proportion to its base, and the coils are nearly horizontal at its neck, all of which gives the appearance of being squashed downward, rather than stretched upward. The overall shape, however, is undoubtedly why it is classified as a Soboba basket. It has a *Bent Finger* Start of Sumac over grass tips, with Sumac over Deer Grass as its primary stitching material.

RMM A1-71 Soboba/Luiseño Bowl
please see Figure 43, page 28,
*Rods, Bundles, and Stitches*

## RMM A1-80 Luiseño Bowl

Museum records describe this basket as "Cahuilla/ Luiseño", suggestive of a circa 1900 Soboba style; i.e. a Cahuilla/Luiseño blend often found at Soboba. Certainly it has a *stretched neck* shape with a whisper of a spittoon rim which was discussed previously. Note that it's belly is quite low (*pear shape*) and the curvature starts to flatten out as its sides approach the neck *(stretched neck shape)*. The coils then start to flare out very slightly near the rim *(spittoon shape)*.

No provenance is available on museum records. However, Cornelius Rumsey did most of his collecting in the 1890–1910 and the basket was well used prior to being acquired. It is 7.7 inches at its widest and is of Sumac over Deer Grass with a pattern of dyed black Juncus. Its "start" is of the *Bent Finger* style of Sumac over grass tips. The pattern is of black Juncus joined diamonds. Workmanship gives evidence of being made by an inexperienced weaver.

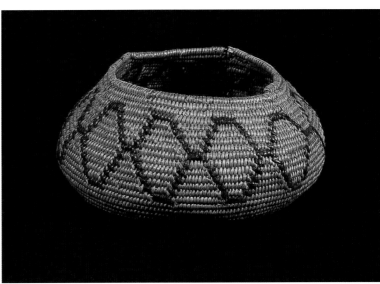

RMM A1-80 Soboba/Luiseño Bowl
as seen in Figure 44, page 29
*Rods, Bundles and Stitches*

RMM, A8-3 Luiseño/Soboba  Bowl
please see Figure 315, page 157, *Rods, Bundles , and Stitches*

### RMM A8-3 Luiseño/Soboba Globular Bowl

There is a question in the mind of the author as to whether this is truly a Luiseño or Soboba bowl. Museum records indicate it is *Cahuilla?, Luiseño?, Soboba Type with mixed Cahuilla and Luiseño traits.* The fact that the stitching material is split Sumac over a Deer Grass foundation with dyed black Juncus pattern material causes it to lean toward a Luiseño origin. Any *one* of the many design motifs might be considered typical of a Luiseño basket, except Luiseño weavers rarely placed such an assortment of motifs on a single basket. This is more of a Cahuilla trait.

A close look at the curvature on the upper several coils suggests that the basket has a *whisper* of the spittoon shape, as seen on many Soboba bowls. It is  9.5 inches in diameter with a rudimentary *stretched neck.* There is a *pierced wad* "start" of Sumac over grass tips. While the remaining coils are Sumac over Deer Grass seed stalks. Cornelius Rumsey collected this bowl circa 1900.

### RMM A83-291 Luiseño/Soboba Storage Bowl

In several previous statements herein, the term *storage basket* was used to describe a large flaring basin-like basket with an open mouth and little or no curvature to the sides. This 10.5 inches diameter bowl is referred to as a storage basket in museum records, presumably because of its large size.  It is rather typical of the *stretched neck* shape found at Soboba. Please note that the *belly* is quite low, almost at the bottom,  and there is a very slight out-curving  at the rim, so typical of baskets created along the *spittoon belt.*

Its two black Juncus bands are common to Luiseño baskets, as is the  *Pierced Wad* "start", with Juncus over Deer Grass tips. Sumac was used on the lower portion, below the pattern, while the upper stitching material is natural Juncus over a clockwise coiling foundation of both shredded Juncus and Deer Grass.

RMM A83-291 Luiseño/Soboba  Storage Bowl
as seen in Figure 352, page 184, *Rods, Bundles, and Stitches*

## RMM A83-292 Soboba/Luiseño Tray

Basketry trays were often used by early Indian people to winnow grass seeds from chaff. After gathering native grass seeds, the lady placed several handfuls in a flat tray and tossed the entire mass into the air, allowing the wind to blow away chaff and dirt yet retain seeds. Quite naturally, the tray must be fairly wide so as to keep seeds from also blowing away. This one is just over 16 inches wide, wide enough!

A *Pierced Wad* type of "start" was used with Sumac over Deer Grass tips. Sumac was used as a primary stitching material on the bottom and near the top, presumably, because of its ability to withstand heavy use. Two black bands of dyed Juncus enclose a band of natural Juncus, which, by contrast, serves as the pattern. Deer Grass forms the clockwise coiling foundation. This basket was collected prior to 1900 in the Soboba area.

RMM A83-292 Luiseño/Soboba Winnowing Tray as pictured in Figure 353, page 185, *Rods, Bundles, and Stitches*

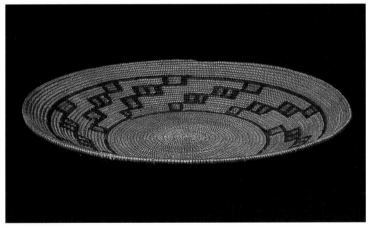

RMM A1236-34 Soboba Winnowing Tray as seen in Figure 43, page 64, *Native American Basketry of Southern California*

## RMM A1236-34 Soboba Winnowing Tray

In 1900, Frank Miller collected this 17 inch diameter, by 3 inch deep winnowing tray, created by Mrs. Jonkulu Apapas of Soboba. Mr. Miller displayed it for many years at his Mission Inn hotel in Riverside. Trays such as this were also used by Indian ladies for their dice gambling games or for winnowing chaff from seeds. In some cases they also parched seeds by placing them in a tray, along with hot wood coals, which were then swished about until the seeds were roasted (parched).

Its pattern contains two black Juncus bands which enclose a rather intricate pattern of 8 sets of up-right spiraling rectangles (sometimes known as *window panes*), 4 rectangles per set. Please note that the first and last rectangle in each spiral is single while the second and third are side-by-side rectangles. Each rectangle *(window pane)* is infilled with pale basal red Juncus. This spiraling pattern of joined rectangles is a rather common theme in Cahuilla and Serrano, but not as common in Luiseño baskets.

This photo has little provenance other than being associated with an assemblage of Northern San Diego County photos taken by Edward Davis presumably in the 1900–1920 period. A copy was given to the author by Nancy Davis Wilson of Mesa Grande, Edward Davis' granddaughter. The lady in the photograph appears to be weaving a Northern San Diego County (? Ipai) basket, and her dwelling is not unlike early willow shelters used by Northern San Diego County Indians.

# CHAPTER 9

# *Pechanga, Pala , and other Luiseño Baskets*

### Basket Descriptions

Baskets represented on the following pages are, unfortunately, not fully representative of Luiseño basketry from southern Riverside and northern San Diego counties. The region generally northeast of Escondido, and south of Temecula, undoubtedly contained a great number of basket makers, many of which were very skilled in artistic presentation. They all spoke a dialect of the Uto-Aztecan (Shoshonean) language and are now known as Luiseños, many of which reside on Indian reservations at 1) La Jolla, 2) Rincon, 3) Pauma, 4) Pala, and 5) Pechanga. Unfortunately, only a very limited number of persons collected baskets from this region between 1890 to 1930 and an even more limited number of baskets found their way into the RMM collections. Mr. Harwood Hall was one of the more prominent collectors and virtually all of those collected by Mr. Hall are very spectacular, but *could not be considered fully representative of the region's basketry*, because Mr. Hall did not collect utility or "*t*ourist*"* baskets.

A search of the Museum's collection reveals 12 baskets attributed to either the Pechanga, Pala, Rincon, or La Jolla region, all of which were collected by one person, Mr. Harwood Hall. Inasmuch as the numbers of such baskets illustrated herein is so limited, preparation of a summary table of characteristics, as was done with the first 56 Luiseño items, (page 77) was not attempted. There is, however, a check list in the appendix, (APP 3-1, page 90) which identifies specific characteristics for each of the 12 basket described in this chapter. That table is intended for the serious student to study individual basket details, but *should not to be used to form conclusions.*

In the following several pages, each of the five BIA (Bureau of Indian Affairs)recognized reservations is discussed. Note that the RMM collection contains none from Pauma, nor from the unrecognized region near Mission San Luis Rey.

### Pechanga

Pechanga is a rather small reservation located a few miles southeast of Temecula in the valley formerly known as the Pauba Ranch, but now known as Rancho California, and by perhaps another half dozen subdivision names. It is best known today for its Pechanga Hotel-Casino and its pending cultural resource center to be located on the former Erle Stanley Gardner ranch (author of literally hundreds of murder mysteries). Tribal officials are slowly but meticulously assembling Southern California Indian basketry and artifact collections to be featured in that center . . . when it is completed. The tribe currently has on display at the tribal offices a portion of the former Justin Farmer collection of some 215 "Mission" baskets, plus a considerable number of local artifacts.

Lamentably, the Riverside Municipal Museum's collection is limited to only 3 baskets from Pechanga, all of which were collected early in the 20th century and donated by Mr. Harwood Hall, a former Superintendent of Sherman Indian Institute. These very fine specimens are large and truly spectacular. It is very possible that more baskets in this collection were made at Pechanga but unfortunately, the collector(s) did not provide the maker's names and left it up to students (like you and me) to guess at their provenance 100 years later. Mr. Hall collected widely throughout Riverside County, either through outright purchase or outright gifts presented to him as Sherman Institute's superintendent. Being a governmental official, professionally associated with Indian people, he had the foresight to collect fairly widely, but unfortunately he did not have the foresight to record complete information about the weaver, and retain it with the basket. Also, Mr. Hall seems to have personified an attitude, very prevalent at the time, which indicated a lack of concern, on the part of most Non- Indians, regarding Indian artists or their art. Lack of provenance on Indian baskets was by no means confined to Luiseño territory; e.g. Sharon Busby, in her Book *Spruce Root Baskets of the Haida and Tlingit (University of Washington Press, 2003)* laments the fact that, prior to very recent years, very little was ever recorded regarding names of Haida and Tlingit weavers of Alaska and Canada. It would seem that even in Alaska and Canada, Non-Indians were quick to collect the creme of Indian art works, but slow to acknowledge the artist's name, or even her (often his) place of origin.

History tells us that on Christmas Day, 1899, a devastating earthquake struck Western Riverside County. Severe damage was reported on most of the local Indian Reservation, albeit much of the entire county suffered damage. It was reported that a family of Indian sisters from the Soboba-Pala-La Jolla region had gathered at Soboba to celebrate Christmas as a family. During the course of the earthquake their building collapsed, killing several of the sisters. Apparently other weavers were also killed. History is silent on their names but if their basketry is any clue, many were spectacular weavers. One of those killed in this 1899 earthquake was a La Jolla lady who created the basket featured on the postage stamp, which is an impetus for this RMM exhibit.

**Pala**

The reservation at Pala has a very interesting history. It is located near the northern end of the Pauma Valley approximately 17 airline miles due north of Escondido, 20 airline miles northeast of Oceanside, and 10 airline miles south of Temecula. In 1903, the US Supreme Court ruled that Ex California Governor Henshaw had more rights to the traditional Indian village of Kupa (now Warner's Hot Springs) than did those Cupeño Indians who occupied the village for dozens of centuries. ERGO, in 1903 the US Army packed up the Indians, and hauled them off to Pala where they were unceremoniously incorporated into a reservation occupied by Luiseños. Although the two peoples were both Shoshonean speakers, their dialects were substantially different, so they could not easily communicate. As a result, Cupeños and Luiseños evolved harmoniously but separately. They both retained their own culture and basketry styles but lived as one united community. Basketry from Pala residents with Cupeño heritage are often referred to as *Cupeño* and not as *Luiseño*, although few basketry students can recognize any appreciable style or pattern differences.

Of the known basket collectors of Pala baskets at the beginning of the 20th century, Harwood Hall was probably the more active. Most of those which he obtained were truly spectacular works of art and a review of his baskets, *alone*, would lead one to a spurious conclusion that all Pala baskets are spectacular. Sans a review of Pala baskets from other collections, it would be misleading to draw any conclusions as to characteristics of Pala Luiseño, or Pala Cupeño baskets. Although a check list of 60 characteristics was prepared, as with the preceding 56 Luiseño baskets, no Summary bar chart was prepared.

Inasmuch as a limited number of baskets from Pechanga, Pala, Rincon, or La Jolla are considered in this chapter, it is quite likely that baskets from these bands were unknowingly included within the first 56 Luiseño baskets, and only those really spectacular Pala baskets are included in this chapter.

## Pauma

This reservation is relatively small and located in the Pauma Valley, south of Pala and north of Rincon. There is currently a casino located on the reservation, nestled at the foothills of Palomar Mountain away from the main highway. No baskets in the RMM collection are listed specifically as being from Pauma.

## Rincon

This reservation is located near the wye junction of State Route 76 and County route S6 at the south end of the Pauma Valley approximately eleven airline miles north of Escondido near the foot of a steep grade leading to Mount Palomar. There is currently an Indian hotel-casino on the reservation but the casino name implies ownership by a Nevada gaming corporation. The reservation borders northern Diegueño (Ipai) territory.

A relatively small number of Rincon baskets are represented in RMM's collection. Basket numbers A8-96 and A8-124 are the only ones directly attributed to this reservation. Both were collected by Harwood Hall and both are quite impressive.

## La Jolla

This is perhaps the southeasternmost Luiseño reservation, it being located in the San Luis Rey River canyon approximately midway between Rincon and Lake Henshaw. It is located in a very steep canyon, bordered by steep brushy hillsides. Camping and RV recreational facilities are its primary source of revenue.

Only a very few baskets are known to have been collected at La Jolla, the most noteworthy is RMM basket, number A8-100, which was selected by the US Postal Service to grace a 37 cent postage stamp. It is this basket which was the impetus for this basketry exhibit catalogue.

## San Luis Rey

Although the term *Luiseño* implies an affiliation with the Mission of San Luis Rey, east of Oceanside, an Indian reservation was never established at, or near the mission proper. There is, today, a small group of Luiseño people residing in this locality who are desirous of federal recognition. There are, undoubtedly Luiseño baskets extant from this region. However, none in the RMM collection are attributed to the vicinity of the old Mission.

**RMM A8-95 Deep Pala Tray**

Harwood Hall collected this very impressive tray on the Pala reservation circa 1900. Its construction, therefore, must have been in the 1890's, well before start of the basket renaissance, or even earlier. Its creator made extensive use of basal red Juncus, which can be harvested in the *Rainbow District,* northwest of the Pala reservation, where Juncus grows to tremendous size with long segments of dark basal red portions. Although floral designs are not common on Luiseño baskets, this one is a spectacular exception. Like many "Mission Baskets" but unlike some by Luiseño weavers, it has a *Knot* "start" of Juncus over a fiber foundation. The primary foundation, however, is Deer Grass. Dr. Moser used a photograph of this basket on the cover of his book *Rods, Bundles, and Stitches* in 1981.

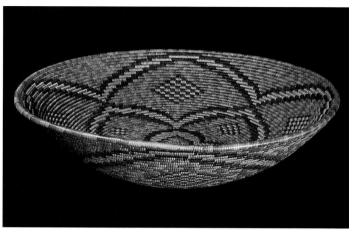

RMM A8-95 Deep Pala Tray as pictured on the cover of *Rods, Bundles, and Stitches, and on Native American Basketry of Southern California*

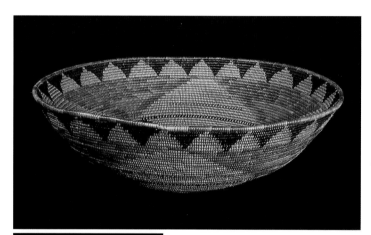

RMM A8-96 Large Rincon Basin
please see Figure 256, page 133 *Rods, Bundles, and Stitches*

**RMM A8-96 Large Rincon Basin**

A collector's tag on this baskets states that it was made at Rincon and its maker was killed in the 1899 earthquake. However, another label states that Harwood Hall collected it in 1896. ERGO, there may be a conflict in dates. In either case it predates 1899.

A *Bent Finger* "start" was used with Sumac over Deer Grass tips. The remainder of the basket has a grass foundation with both Sumac and Juncus as stitching material. The pattern has a number of surprises. First, there is one coil of alternating black Juncus/Sumac at the tips of the flower petals, followed by another several coils further out. The latter has both red Juncus/Sumac and black Juncus/Sumac. At the 9:00 o'clock position, there is a third partial coil of red Juncus/Sumac. The latter is believed (by the author) to be a pattern anomaly, which is not uncommon on Luiseño baskets. The maker signed the basket using a tiny black stitch at the 8:00 o'clock position immediately below the outer row of triangles.

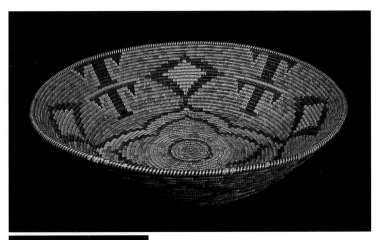

## RMM A8-97 Large Pala Basin

Harwood Hall collected this very impressive basketry on the Pala Rez (Reservation) in 1900. It is one of the very few in which he recorded the name of the maker; i.e. Sarah Moronga. Mr. Hall must have been very favorably impressed with basal red Juncus as a base material because, like many of the baskets he collected, this one has basal red Juncus as the primary stitching material over a Deer Grass foundation. As used in this case, basal red Juncus creates a very pleasing mottled appearance.

Note the multiples of 4 in the pattern. However, the weaver's use of Sumac as an accent material is very subtle, including the 5 coils of Sumac plus basal red Juncus triangles at the base, Note also the black band at the base and alternating black Juncus/Sumac stitches at the rim. The author has avoided any wild guesses as to meaning of the stacked "T's".

RMM A8-97 Large Wide Pala Basin
please see Figure 42, page 64, *Native American Basketry of Southern California*

## RMM A8-98 Large Pechanga Basin

Like basket number RMM A8-96, on a previous page, museum records show that Harwood Hall collected this 17 inch wide basin at Pechanga circa 1890, and the weaver, who remains nameless, was reportedly killed in the 1899 Christmas Day earthquake. Although the weaver was from Pechanga, the pattern shows very heavy Cahuilla influence; i.e. extensive use of dyed black Juncus, moderate use of basal red Juncus, a sparse field of Sumac, and use of eagles/condors and animals, both positive and negative. Luiseño weavers rarely used zoomorphic motifs or abstract motifs as in this case. Note also the pattern anomaly; i.e. a black stripe through the red diamond at the 11:00 o'clock position.

The weaver used a *Bent Finger* "start" with Juncus over a core of Deer Grass tips. Its primary foundation is also Deer Grass and the base stitching material is Sumac.

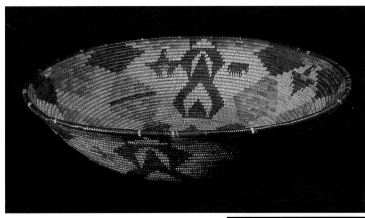

RMM A8-98 Large Pechanga Basin
as shown in Figure 25, page 21, *Rods, Bundles, and Stitches*

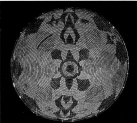

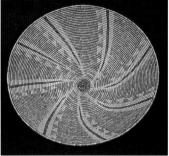

RMM A8-99 Deep
Pechanga Basin
see cover, *Native
American Basketry of
Southern California*

### RMM A8-99 Deep Pechanga Basin

This is another of the Harwood Hall baskets which he collected around 1900. Museum records indicate it is from the "Pechanga-Pala area". The rim is 17 inches wide and is in excellent condition. The late Dr. Chris Moser selected this as one of three baskets to be featured on the cover of his book *Native American Basketry of Southern California*, 1993. Of all the Luiseño baskets in the RMM collection, this is the only one with *Whirlwinds;* i.e. with spiraling lines radiating from the center. This is a trait usually associated with Serrano baskets. It is also the only one with a solid black center, as is so often the case with Pima (Akimel O'odham) baskets from Arizona. Its "start" is of the *Bent Finger* style using Sumac over a core of Deer Grass tips. The remainder of the basket is of basal red Juncus over a grass foundation. The whirlwind spirals are black Juncus outlined in Sumac.

### RMM A8-100 Wide La Jolla Tray

In the year 2002, Dr. Christopher Moser, then Curator of Anthropology at RMM, interested the US Postal Service in featuring an Indian basket on a 37 cent postage stamp. He submitted photos of this specific basket and it was selected to join 9 other Indian art pieces for an August 2004 issue commemorating opening of the new NMAI (National Museum of the American Indian) museum in Washington D.C. Harwood Hall collected the basket on the La Jolla Reservation and noted that the maker, whom he failed to name, was killed in an earthquake in 1899. This suggests that it was made in the 1890's or earlier. Like many of the baskets collected by Harwood Hall, it has extensive basal red Juncus, with patterns of black Juncus, infilled by lighter Sumac. Museum records suggest that the design is a 5 petal flower with water bugs. The "start" is of the *Bent Finger* type with Juncus over Yucca fiber. Its body is of basal red Juncus over a grass foundation.

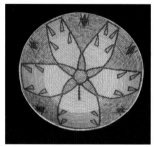

RMM A8-100 Wide La Jolla
Tray
see cover of this Treatise, and
Figure 95 page 69,
*Native American Basketry of
Southern California.*

**RMM A8-104 Large Pechanga Basin**
A close comparison between this and basket RMM A8-98, on a previous page, would suggest that there was a relationship between the weaver(s) of these two baskets. Both were from Pechanga, both used black motifs very vividly, both used black and negative eagles (or condors), both used zoomorphic motifs, both used the *Bent Finger* start with Deer Grass tips for a core, both used stylized black Juncus motifs, and both incorporated a solid black rim. Unlike the previous basket, this one has the rattle end of a Rattlesnake near the rim, 8 lightning bolts, and a rather fat black anthropomorph (stylized human). It's a shame we don't know the weaver's name.

Harwood Hall collected the basket during the 1890's. It is interesting to note that the primary stitching material on the bottom is Sumac over Deer Grass, whereas the upper portion is Juncus over Deer Grass. A supposition is made that the Sumac was placed on the bottom to withstand anticipated heavy wear. ERGO, the basket may have been made for heavy use, not specifically to sell.

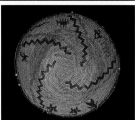

RMM A8-104 Large Pechanga Basin
as seen in Figure 26, page 21, *Rods, Bundles, and Stitches*

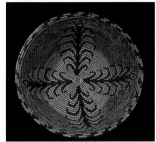

RMM A8-110 Large and Deep Pala Bowl
as pictured in Figure 87, page 68, *Native American Basketry of Southern California*

**RMM A8-110 Large and Deep Pala Basin**
Some baskets fairly scream that they want to be studied in detail. Such is the case here. Mr. Hall collected it 1900–1910 on the Pala Rez, but neglected to name names or places. The basket has some of the characteristics of basket RMM A8-104, above, except that the latter was collected in Pechanga (only a dozen miles away). The weaver utilized a *Knot* "start" of Sumac over a core of Deer Grass tips. Then, like RMM A8-104, Sumac over Deer Grass makes up the bottom, after which the weaver used basal red Juncus over grass for the base stitching material.

An interesting feature of the basket is its shape and rim style. Its sides are relatively steep and of Juncus until it reaches the rim. Suddenly the last two coils flare out very dramatically and consist of alternating Sumac and black Juncus. This style of rim is very unique and was seldom, if ever, used on a Luiseño basket. The stylized corn plant, as well as the flare-out rim suggest the weaver had strong ties to the Cahuilla people.

## RMM A8-118 Deep Pala Basin/Bowl

During the late 1800's and early 1900's, Harwood Hall, as superintendent of the U.S. Bureau of Indian Affairs' Sherman Institute in Riverside, traveled widely throughout Southern California and collected some very prime examples of Indian art. This basket is a fine example. His records state it was created on the Pala reservation but gives no names or dates, other than early 1900's. Based upon its shape it could have been intended as a small burden basket, a storage basket, or merely a piece of fine art. Note the excellent control the weaver exerted on its design, plus the subtle use of vertical *wavy* red Juncus lines, which could suggest heat waves.

Interestingly, the weaver used both clipped and Bound Under Fag End Stitches (BUFES), a trait quite rare among Luiseños but very common in Desert Cahuilla baskets. The "start" is of the *Bent Finger* style with Sumac over grass tips. Sumac over Deer Grass is the primary material with patterns of basal red and dyed black Juncus.

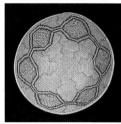

RMM A8-118 Deep Pala Basin
also shown in Figure 339, page 180,
*Rods, Bundles and Stitches*

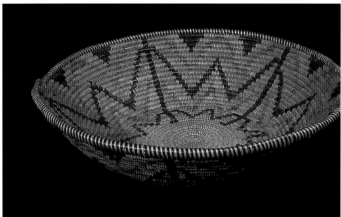

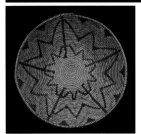

RMM A8-122 Deep and Wide
Pala Basin
Please see Figure 97, page 69,
*Native American Basketry of
Southern California*

## RMM A8-122 Deep and Wide Pala Basin

Museum records indicate this basket was collected by Harwood Hall circa 1900 on the Pala reservation and is "Luiseño or ? Cupeño". Inasmuch as Cupeño people were not relocated to Pala until 1903, there is either a question as to its collection date or as to its possible Cupeño affiliation. Because so few Cupeño baskets are extant, little can be said positively regarding their traits. It does, however, resemble those created by the Cahuilla.

The weaver used a *Bent Finger* "start" with Sumac over Deer Grass tips. The relatively small bottom is Sumac over Deer Grass, which changes to Juncus over grass on its sides. Note the interesting use of basal red Juncus forming concentric 10 pointed stars, and the left handed feet on the radial black Juncus "spokes". Note also the alternating rim stitches of Sumac and dyed black Juncus, a feature reasonable rare to Luiseño baskets.

## RMM A8-124 Large and Shallow Rincon Basin

Mr. Harwood Hall collected this basket circa 1900 on the Rincon Rez at the southern end of the Pauma Valley near the Luiseño/Diegueño (Ipai) frontier approximately 10 air miles north of Escondido. The extensive use of basal red Juncus with minimal dyed black Juncus suggests a close affiliation with Ipai weavers who also used minimal black Juncus, preferring instead, to use substantial amounts of natural or basal red Juncus for both the field and pattern. It differs from most Ipai baskets in that the latter tend to use larger geometric pattern motifs, while this basket tends toward horizontal bands rather than isolated motifs. Ipai baskets also rarely have a checker board of black Juncus and tan Sumac.

This basket's creator utilized a *Knot* "start" of Sumac over Deer Grass tips. The remainder of the base is of Sumac over Deer Grass seed stalks. Varigated Juncus was used on the sides leading to the three coil checker board of alternating stitches of black Juncus and Sumac. That checker board ends one coil from the rim.

RMM A8-124 Large and Shallow Rincon Basin see Figure 124, page 65, *Rod, Bundles, and Stitches*

## RMM A8-128 Small La Jolla Gift Bowl

This really nice little gift basket was collected 1900–1908 on the La Jolla Rez by Harwood Hall but has a number of traits that may be atypical for that area. First, most Luiseño baskets do not have quite this many spiraling lines from the base to the top. Second, most baskets from La Jolla do not use this much black with so little red Juncus, and last, this basket has both clipped and BUFES (Bound Under Fag End Stitches). The first several coils exhibit the BUFES, after which fag ends are clipped. Its "start" is of the *Bent Finger* style with Sumac over grass tips. The remainder of the field is of Sumac over a grass foundation

The almost perfect bowl shape is characteristic of Ipai (Diegueño) weavers. The one basal and two peripheral bands are very characteristically Luiseño, and spiral lines suggest Cahuilla or Serrano lineages, not Luiseño or Ipai.

RMM A8-128 Small La Jolla Gift Bowl see Figure 101, page 69, *Native American Basketry of Southern California*

***Ramona Balenzuela- master basket maker***

Ramona Balenzuela was an Ipai lady from Mesa Grande, approximately 60 miles northeast of San Diego. She was a master basket maker and created a number of very spectacular baskets in the Ipai (Northern Diegueño) style. The Basket on Mrs. Balenzuela's right is in the Riverside Municipal Museum collection. One of her very fine baskets was obtained from the author by, and now resides in, the Pechanga tribal cultural center. The photo is from the author's private collection.

# CHAPTER 10

# *Summary*

**Impetus for this Exhibit**

In 2002, the late Dr. Christopher "Chris" Moser, RMM's Curator of anthropology submitted photos and documents of a Luiseño basket to the US Postal Service (USPS) requesting that it be included in a commemorative pane of ten 37 cent stamps, which the USPS planned to issue celebrating the opening of the Smithsonian's new National Museum of the American Indian museum in the National Mall, Washington D.C. The basket selected by the USPS was item A8-100, one collected by Mr. Harwood Hall on the La Jolla reservation. Accession documents indicate the unnamed weaver died in an earthquake which devastated northern San Diego and southern Riverside counties on Christmas Day, 1899.

To celebrate this stamp issue, the Riverside Municipal Museum mounted an October, 2004 to March, 2005, exhibit, entitled "Timeless Beauty: Objects from Luiseño Daily Life". That exhibit featured a great number of Luiseño baskets from RMM's substantial basket collection. This catalogue presumes that few basketry students ever have the opportunity to closely inspect basket characteristics and provenance in a major museum, or to closely study baskets in an exhibit case. Therefore, the author has presented herein a check list of 60 different characteristics which may, or may not, be present in each basket. Although the narrative accompanying each basket is rather cursory, it is offered in the hopes that the reader can better relate to a specific basket. It was the initial hope of the author that a series of generic characteristics might be defined for Luiseño baskets. That hope was only partially fulfilled, as explained in more detail later in this chapter.

It is regrettable that the moving force behind this commemorative stamp and the resulting exhibition is no longer with us. It is therefore the desire of this author that this catalogue be dedicated to Dr. Christopher "Chris" Moser.

**History of "Mission Indian" Title**

The terms *"Mission Indian"* and *"Mission Basket"* are used frequently in this text, and a distinction was made between the term *Mission*, as a Catholic church related facility, and *"Mission"* as it relates to a tribe of Indians in Southern California. To explain the nexus between these two terms, a rather lengthy history of Southern California was given in chapter 1, which addressed origins of the various tribal names still used in Southern California.

Summarized very briefly, the Spanish missionaries who arrived in what is now California in 1769, laid claim to all lands and people as subjects of the Spanish crown and the Catholic church. Indians within the territorial boundaries of each mission were assigned a name associated with the specific mission. Those mission-related names survived until the present and are still used to designate "Mission Baskets" from Southern California.

## Three Sub-groups of Luiseños

Very frequently, "Mission" baskets are defined in more detail as either Diegueño, Luiseño, Juaneño, Gabrielino, Fernandeño, Serrano, Cahuilla, or Cupeño. When an even more detailed study is desired, a more definitive title is often applied; e.g. *Santa Ysabel* Diegueño, or *Pala* Luiseño, or *Soboba* Luiseño, or *Mountain* Cahuilla. Unfortunately, good provenance (information as to the weaver's name or locale, date of creation, etc) is usually not available from museum records. In the RMM collection, 56 of the 76 baskets discussed herein have no reliable provenance and thus were considered *generic Luiseño,* which is the first of three sub-groups in this treatise. Soboba is the second sub-groups and was selected because Soboba, while not actually within Luiseño territory, represents a locale where Cahuilla, Serrano, Gabrielino, Luiseño, and even some Diegueño persons lived as one semi-homogenous enclave. Over the years, their basketry assumed certain diagnostic shapes, to the extent that some basketry students define a certain shape as a *Soboba style.* The third sub-group includes baskets from Pechanga, Pala, Rincon, and La Jolla. The RMM collection contains 12 very spectacular baskets in this group. Unfortunately, all 12 were collected by the same person circa 1900 and thus are not necessarily representative of basketry from these four reservations. **Please see *Unintentional Bias*, later in this chapter**.

## "Mission" Baskets

At the time of European contact (1769), two dramatically different language stocks and a dozen or more dialects were spoken in Southern California. However, there was no dramatic differences in their basketry styles and collectors, over the years conjoined all Southern California baskets under the one title, "Mission Baskets". Virtually all "Mission Baskets" are of the coiled technique and contain a foundation of either Deer Grass *(Muhlenbergia rigins)* and/or split Juncus *(Juncus textilis).* Stitching material is either of Juncus *(Juncus textilis)* or Sumac *(Rhus trilobata).* On very rare occasions, Yucca root ( *Yucca brevifolia,* aka Joshua tree) was used for red pattern material. On even more rare occasions, black pattern elements were created using fibers from the Devils Claw *(Martynia sp.)* pod, a low desert plant used extensively in Arizona and New Mexico. Juncus is (was) used either in its natural tan/buff state, its basal red state, or dyed black. Luiseño baskets are famous for their pattern motifs of dyed black Juncus on a light tan colored base of Sumac. A review of Table 1, page 77, indicates occurrence frequency of Juncus, Sumac, or other fibers.

## Weaving Techniques.

With only a very few minor exceptions, all Southern California Indian baskets were constructed using a coiling technique; i.e. a thin mass of Deer Grass seed stalks, or pieces of Juncus, was squeezed into a thin rope-like bundle, then wrapped with either Juncus or Sumac weaver strands. These weaver strands secured the rope-like bundle, or coil, to an underlying coil. Each coil spirals outward, similar to coil springs in an old fashioned clock. Patterns were applied using either a red or black stitching material, in contrast to the basic tan field material (either natural tan Juncus or honey hued Sumac).

**Unintentional Biases ( *"Collector bias"*)**

*Author's note:*
*Use of the term Bias, is often suggestive of a mean-spirited prejudice for, or against, something and thus is necessarily bad. NO SUCH IMPLICATION IS IMPLIED HERE! A bias can enter any discussion, topic, or subject, regardless of its nature and, in some cases, as is the case here, can be beneficial. In the course of learning . . . learning anything . . . it is imperative that the student be aware of hidden biases, or **hidden agendas**. Recognizing a bias may be extremely valuable and often helps avoid some very painful pitfalls.*

In the course of inspecting the baskets included herein, it became evident that basketry students, such as the author, often have inherent semi-firm ideas as to what constitutes a Luiseño basket, based upon either; 1) personal experience, 2) personal inspections of baskets, sometimes hundreds of such baskets, 3) reading treatises by "experts", 4) hear-say, or 5) just plain gut-feel. Although reading a discourse based upon a detailed study of baskets from a respectable collection, by an experienced author, may seem to be a very scholarly approach, baskets in many, if not most, large collections often have a built-in bias that is not outwardly apparent.

Such is the case at the Riverside Municipal Museum with certain portions of the collection. For example, twelve of the baskets discussed in chapter 9, above, are listed as being from Pechanga, Pala, Rincon, or La Jolla. Unfortunately, all were collected by the same person; viz. Mr. Harwood Hall who was not substantially different from most serious collectors. He had certain likes, dislikes, preferences, and perhaps unrecognized biases. He was apparently a devotee of large basin shaped very colorful, very "busy" multichrome baskets. Please note that 11 of the 12, baskets described in Chapter 9 are very "showy" and of the large basin shape, while only one is small and globular, even that one is relatively showy. Inasmuch as all baskets described in chapter 9 were collected by the same person, around the same time period, suggests to the author, and hopefully to the reader, that they merely represent the style of basket favored by that one person, and, in no way defines all baskets from this region.

In contrast, 29 of the 56 baskets (over 50%) described in chapter 7 were collected by Mr. and Mrs. Cornelius Rumsey, and seem to run the gamut from very spectacular to very utilitarian. This array tells us a lot about the collectors and implies that they were interested in virtually all the various styles. ERGO, their collection can be studied with a greater degree of confidence than can those in Chapter 9.

The above phenomenon of bias in collecting undoubtedly occurs in most, if not all major collections or museums. Fortunately the RMM cataloguing method assigns a customized prefix number to each item referring to a specific donor; e.g. *A1-xxx* indicates that the item was donated by Cornelius Rumsey, while *A8* -xxx tells us Harwood Hall was the donor. A student can therefore tell at a glance if there is a likelihood of *"Collector Bias"*, particularly if there are a number of items collected by one person and they are all similar in appearance, date, locale, or in some other matter. Most museums use their own customized numbering system; e.g. Date of Accession (1956-xxyy), Tribal Affiliation (Chu xxyz), Locale (NA, Cal. Pai. xxyz), etc. Such systems make it harder to spot *Collector Biases*. They do, however, offer other advantages not available with the RMM system.

**Collection Dates**

From a technical view point, date of manufacture for a given basket is of extreme interest to a serious basketry student. In most cases, information on accession cards is scanty, at best. The collector might have noted when it was first obtained, or some other bit of information which allows the current student to synthesize a probable construction date or era. For example, some baskets have a notation that the creator died in the 1899 Christmas Day earthquake, which tells us that basket is pre-1899. Approximately how many years before 1899 can sometimes be judged based upon wear. Collection dates are also important because they give a *"No-Later-Than"* clue as to a creation date. To put dates into prospective the reader should bear in mind that during the period 1769 to 1835 (+/-), Spanish Catholic missionaries were busy eradicating Indian culture and replacing it with one based upon the Catholic church and Spanish crown. The reader must recognize that 1769 was in the waning stages of the Spanish Inquisition and the people occupying California were part of the *Conquistadors;* the Spaniards being the *Conquistador-ors,* and the Indians *Conquistador-ees.* Indian basket making was not acceptable to the *conquistador-ors* because it represented a native culture that had to be eradicated. Therefore, a pitifully few were retained in any collections. After 1835, the old missions were abandoned and their Indian serfs scattered to the 4 winds. Few Indians were left to make baskets, even if they still remembered how. After 1850, when California became a member of the United States, Indians were valued primarily as laborers or as objects to be bought and sold on the auction block every Monday morning in downtown Los Angeles. Few were valued as artists. Metal pots and pans had supplanted basket for household uses, and beside, *who wanted a remnant of an antiquated primitive culture?*

During the late 19th century; i.e. prior to about 1890, most Indian baskets were made for home use, and very few made for sale. However, starting in the late 1890's or around the turn of the 20th century (1900) Non-Indians suddenly became interested in salvaging remnants of that primitive culture they were busily stomping out. That interest increased into a fever pitch into the 1920's, only to die again, a victim of the great depression after 1929.

Documenting the approximate creation date of a basket is a good measure by which to judge the amount of external influence in its design/construction. Quite obviously a basket collected in 1900 was made prior to 1900 and thus very likely represents a style-technique only minimally influenced by *outsiders*. It is quite evident that a well worn storage or utility basket collected in the 1890's, represents an item created well before 1890, with little or no Non-Indian influence. Collection dates are therefore of keen interest to students of traditional basketry styles and designs. Very fortunately, many in the Cornelius Rumsey collection fall into that category.

**Local Differences**

The reader's attention is directed to chapters 7 (Generic Luiseño), 8 (Soboba) and 9 (Pechanga, Pala, Rincon, and La Jolla) for discussions regarding local differences in basketry styles. Attention is also directed to Tables APP. 1- 1thru 6, Tables APP. 2-1, and Table APP. 3-1&2 in the Appendix hereto. These tables list, in a comparative format, 60 different characteristics for each basket described in the text. If a reader is interested in a specific characteristic; such as the  type of "start" *(e.g. Knot, Bent Finger, or Pierced Wad),* or materials used, etc. these tables will be of assistance.

The purpose of subdividing Luiseño baskets into three categories, and listing them as *1) Generic Luiseños, 2) Soboba, and 3) Pechanga, Pala, Rincon, and La Jolla,* is that the first 56 baskets are more-or-less generic with little or no provenance. In the second case, Soboba is an isolated enclave where Cahuilla, Serrano, Gabrielino, Luiseño, and even a few Diegueño people lived together on one reservation. Their baskets reflect this hybridization of different cultures. The third group represents the four reservations of Pechanga, Pala, Rincon, and La Jolla. Baskets in this group were all collected by one person. Therefore, combining all 76 baskets into one category would very likely result in spurious conclusions.

### Generic Luiseño Baskets

RMM records, as are many museum records, often unclear as to the tribal origin of a specific items. Some records contain a statement that the item is *"attributed to"* or *"similar to"*, or *"possibly . . .",* or some other less than emphatic narrative. Prior to describing a specific basket, the author examined it quite carefully and in most instances concurred in, or at least quoted, the statement on its accession document. Where a question arose in the author's mind, a statement was made to that effect on the associated description herein.

In general, the 56 baskets in this category ranged from flat trays, to large open basins, to burden/storage baskets. Most, however, did not vary widely in weaving styles, patterns or materials. Tables APP 1-1 through 6, in the appendix hereto, indicate which of 60 characteristics are applicable to each basket. Data from those tables were then summarized into Table 1, page 77. The purpose of Table 1 is to graphically illustrate the occurrence frequency of each of those 60 traits. Such a summary table was not prepared for Soboba or the other tribes because of the small number of samples, or the *unintentional bias* associated with the baskets in the other categories.

### Summary Table

A few notes regarding data included in the Summary, Table 1:
The column entitled "NO." indicates the number of baskets which exhibit the characteristic listed. For example, there are 9 baskets classified as trays and 25 referred to herein as Basin/Bowl. As to bottoms, 39 have flat and the bottom is concave on 17 of them. The next column heading, "%" , lists the percentage of total that exhibit that particular characteristic. Please note there were 56 generic Luiseño specimens under study. However, some exhibited examples of two or more characteristics; e.g. in category 3, SIDES, there are 82 listing under the "NO." column. This means that some baskets have sides that both flare out and curve, as in a wide basin shape. Therefore, the numerals in the "%" column do not necessarily add to 100%. Conversely, some categories have minimal frequency; e.g. only 6 of the 56 have an anomaly and even less, 5, have a signature. Therefore, the numeral in the "%" column are for general reference only and the relative length of the horizontal bar is the critical feature of Table 1. The following addresses each of the 14 general features in Table 1.

1. **SHAPE:** By far the greatest shape found in this collection, 45%, are classified herein as either a bowl or basin (like a wash basin or gold dust pan). A lesser percentage, 25%, are storage or burden baskets, and 16% are trays. This range of shapes probably reflects collector bias more than any preferences on the part of the weaver.

2. **BOTTOM:** Nearly 70 percent of all bottoms are flat with 30% concave (curved downward). This is in contrast to Diegueño baskets whose bottoms tend to be mostly concave rather than flat.

3. **SIDES:** Inasmuch as Basin/Bowls are the predominant shape, sides are predominantly flaring (84%) with most of them (55%)also curving, rather than being straight. Please note that only one has a pronounced shoulder and none has a protruding "belly".

4. **TERMINAL:** Because of rim damage, it was not possible to study terminals on all baskets. Of those terminals which are in evidence, 30 are rather blunt, being under 2 inches long. Only 14 terminals are greater than 2 inches in length.

5. **BACK STITCH:** Only 46 of the 56 baskets have visible terminals where back stitching could be studied. Of these, 8 have no back stitches, 24 have 1-5 back stitches, and 14 have more than 5. In several cases, back stitches are evident but the terminal is inconclusive.

6. **"START":** One of the surprising results of this study was finding that most Luiseño baskets exhibit a *"Bent Finger" or "Pierced Wad"* type of start rather than the *Knot* style, which is rather common in Diegueño baskets.

   *Perhaps the most surprising feature* of this entire assessment is the fact that 54% of the baskets contain a "start" foundation of tips of Deer Grass seed stalks rather than fiber, which some students, including the author, believed to be the primary foundation material in "starts".

7. **FAG ENDS:** Please note that 93% of the generic Luiseño baskets studied herein have the BUFES, (Bound Under Fag End Stitch). Only one has clipped fag ends and one has both clipped and BUFES. This comes as no surprise because use of the BUFES is very diagnostic of Luiseño baskets.

8. **FOUNDATION:** Of the 56 baskets under study, 53 (95%) have a Deer Grass foundation and only five, 9%, make use of split Juncus reeds.

9. **STITCHING MATERIAL:** Nearly 79 % of the generic Luiseño baskets included in this study have stitching material of Sumac, with 13% using Juncus, and only 7% using both.

10. **PATTERN MATERIAL:** It comes as no surprise that 95% of all baskets studied have black Juncus as a pattern material. Surprising however, is the fact that only 10 (19%) have basal red Juncus in their pattern. The spread regarding complexity of pattern motifs showed that 61% have a mildly complex pattern, 23% have an austere pattern, and only 9% have what is considered herein as a complex pattern.

11. **PATTERN ORIENTATION:** Over two thirds (68%) of the baskets have a horizontally oriented pattern, as compared with a rather even split of other orientations.

12. **MOTIFS:** Approximately 80% of the pattern motifs are geometric in nature, as contrasted to floral, natural, or stylized shapes. Of the 56 specimens, only one has a zoomorphic motif (animal or bird) and only 2 contain an anthropomorph (human). Approximately 52% have one or more black horizontal band.

13. **ANOMALY:** An anomaly is a break or a feature in the pattern that is not natural but was placed there by an experienced weaver. Only 6 baskets contain an anomaly.

14. **SIGNATURE:** Some weavers signed their art work with a peculiar stitch or series of stitches. Such signatures are often not readily visible and when found are not recognized as a signature. Five baskets have such a signature.

**Summary Table 1**
Summary of 56 Luiseño Baskets
Southern California Luiseño Baskets
Frequency of Characteristics

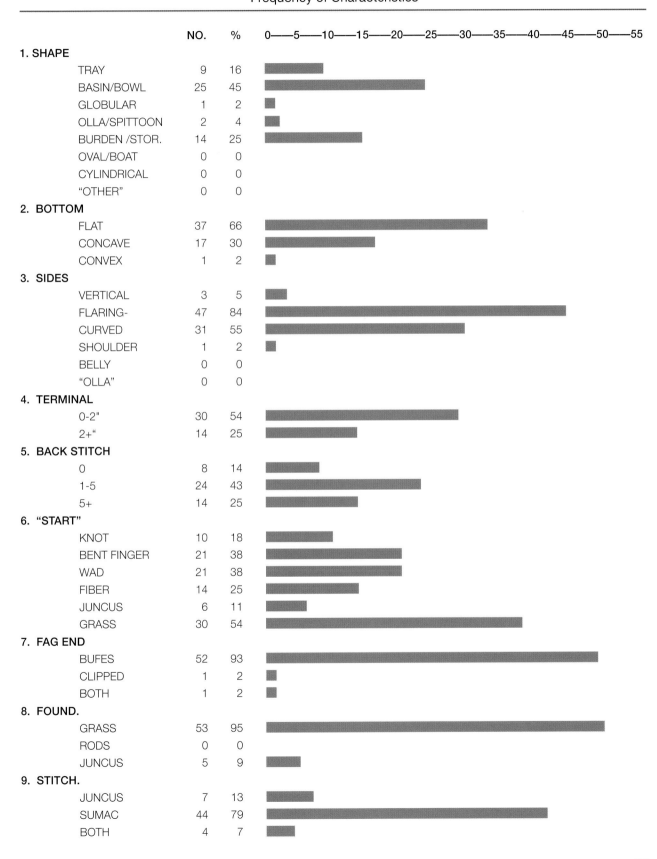

| | NO. | % |
|---|---|---|
| **1. SHAPE** | | |
| TRAY | 9 | 16 |
| BASIN/BOWL | 25 | 45 |
| GLOBULAR | 1 | 2 |
| OLLA/SPITTOON | 2 | 4 |
| BURDEN /STOR. | 14 | 25 |
| OVAL/BOAT | 0 | 0 |
| CYLINDRICAL | 0 | 0 |
| "OTHER" | 0 | 0 |
| **2. BOTTOM** | | |
| FLAT | 37 | 66 |
| CONCAVE | 17 | 30 |
| CONVEX | 1 | 2 |
| **3. SIDES** | | |
| VERTICAL | 3 | 5 |
| FLARING- | 47 | 84 |
| CURVED | 31 | 55 |
| SHOULDER | 1 | 2 |
| BELLY | 0 | 0 |
| "OLLA" | 0 | 0 |
| **4. TERMINAL** | | |
| 0-2" | 30 | 54 |
| 2+" | 14 | 25 |
| **5. BACK STITCH** | | |
| 0 | 8 | 14 |
| 1-5 | 24 | 43 |
| 5+ | 14 | 25 |
| **6. "START"** | | |
| KNOT | 10 | 18 |
| BENT FINGER | 21 | 38 |
| WAD | 21 | 38 |
| FIBER | 14 | 25 |
| JUNCUS | 6 | 11 |
| GRASS | 30 | 54 |
| **7. FAG END** | | |
| BUFES | 52 | 93 |
| CLIPPED | 1 | 2 |
| BOTH | 1 | 2 |
| **8. FOUND.** | | |
| GRASS | 53 | 95 |
| RODS | 0 | 0 |
| JUNCUS | 5 | 9 |
| **9. STITCH.** | | |
| JUNCUS | 7 | 13 |
| SUMAC | 44 | 79 |
| BOTH | 4 | 7 |

77

**Table 1 (cont.)**
Summary of 56 Luiseño Baskets
Frequency of Characteristics

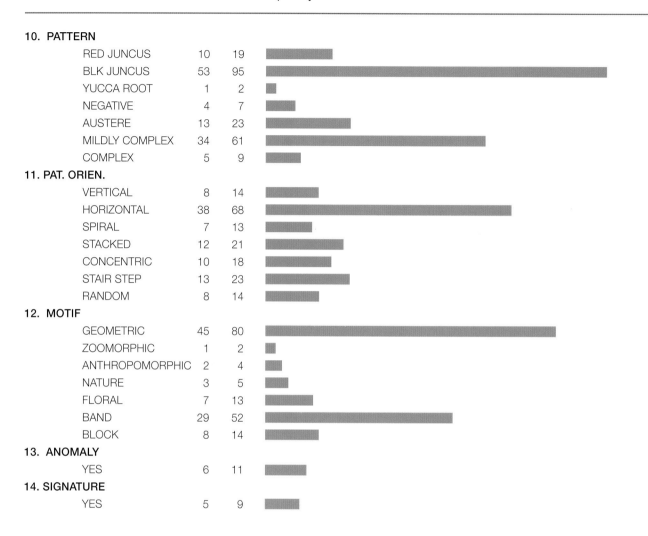

| | | | |
|---|---|---|---|
| **10. PATTERN** | | | |
| RED JUNCUS | 10 | 19 | |
| BLK JUNCUS | 53 | 95 | |
| YUCCA ROOT | 1 | 2 | |
| NEGATIVE | 4 | 7 | |
| AUSTERE | 13 | 23 | |
| MILDLY COMPLEX | 34 | 61 | |
| COMPLEX | 5 | 9 | |
| **11. PAT. ORIEN.** | | | |
| VERTICAL | 8 | 14 | |
| HORIZONTAL | 38 | 68 | |
| SPIRAL | 7 | 13 | |
| STACKED | 12 | 21 | |
| CONCENTRIC | 10 | 18 | |
| STAIR STEP | 13 | 23 | |
| RANDOM | 8 | 14 | |
| **12. MOTIF** | | | |
| GEOMETRIC | 45 | 80 | |
| ZOOMORPHIC | 1 | 2 | |
| ANTHROPOMORPHIC | 2 | 4 | |
| NATURE | 3 | 5 | |
| FLORAL | 7 | 13 | |
| BAND | 29 | 52 | |
| BLOCK | 8 | 14 | |
| **13. ANOMALY** | | | |
| YES | 6 | 11 | |
| **14. SIGNATURE** | | | |
| YES | 5 | 9 | |

**Soboba Baskets**

A review of the Tribal Boundary Map, Figure 2, page 7, will show that the reservation of Soboba is located well outside of what is generally considered Luiseño territory; i.e. well into Cahuilla country. However, because of hybridization of tribal affiliations at this rez, some basketry bowls took on a very specific shape early in the 20th century. Many of the items made for sale are of the *squat bowl* shape with a pronounced *Belly;* i.e. the widest point is very low on the side, often not much above the 1/4 mark. Also, inasmuch as Soboba is at the northern end of the "Spittoon Belt" some of the bowls tend to have either a slight flaring-out at the rim (semi-spittoon shaped), or what has been described earlier as a *stretched neck.* Soboba baskets with a shape other than a bowl, are often hard to distinguish from those created by Cahuilla, Serrano, or even Luiseño weavers.

*A word of caution!* The reader must be careful not to classify all Soboba baskets as having a *stretched neck* or a *spittoon rim.* Many of the weavers at this reservation were of Cahuilla or Serrano lineage and followed classic Cahuilla or Serrano styles. Also, some baskets with a noticeable flaring-out at the rim; i.e. an "Olla" shape, might rightfully be attributed to Ipai or Tipai (Diegueño) weavers from the Julian-Cuyamaca-Laguna Mountain region.

**Pechanga, Pala, Rincon, and La Jolla**

*Again, a word of caution!* All 12 baskets attributed to this region and included in this exhibit were collected around the turn of the 20th century by Mr. Harwood Hall and are truly spectacular pieces of art. A study of just those 12 items would lead to a very serious and spurious conclusion. The only true conclusion that should be drawn is that Harwood Hall was impressed with these baskets . . . *Nothing more!* Because the only Pechanga, Pala, Rincon or La Jolla baskets in this exhibit were all collected by one person, the reader is cautioned not to draw any conclusions other than to admire these baskets for their beauty.

***Mrs. Lugo winnowing chaff***

Winnowing trays were used both for gathering seeds in the field and for winnowing chaff away from the seeds. In this photograph, Mrs. Lugo placed a basketry gathering tray under a bush and then beat the branches to dislodge seeds, which collected in the tray. Although not easily seen, Mrs. Lugo held a s*eed beater* in her right hand. That beater looks similar to a tennis racquet and was hastily made, used, and discarded. This Edward Davis photo is from the author's collection.

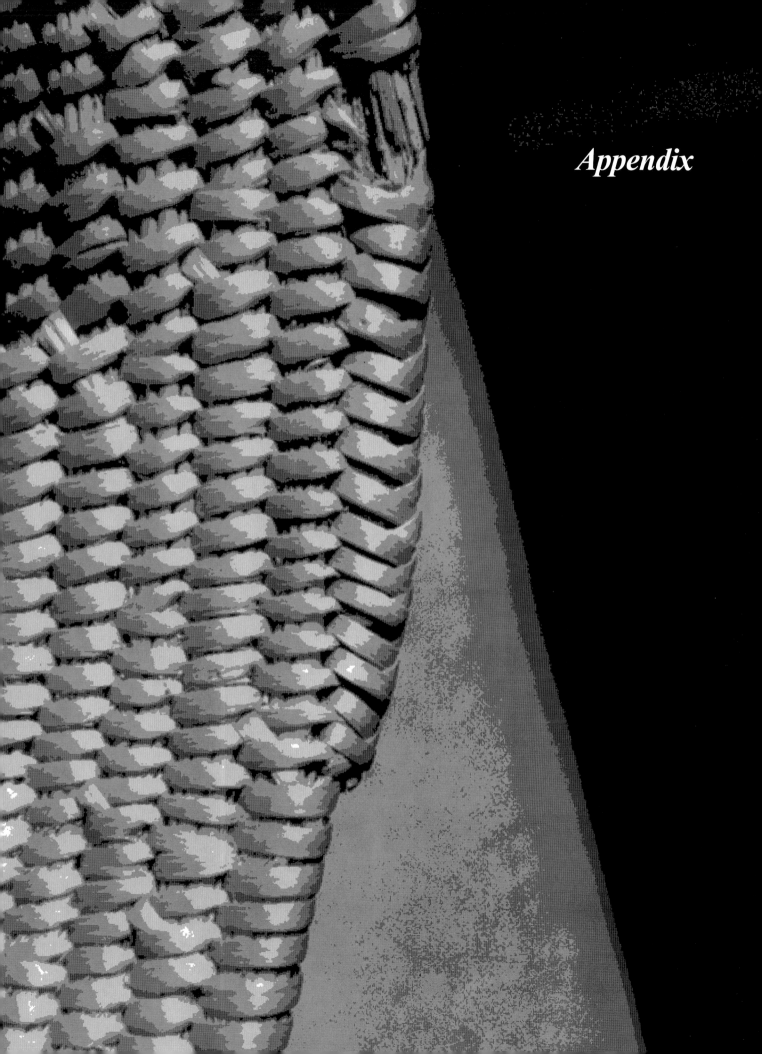

*Appendix*

**Mr. and Mrs. Victorianno of the Soboba people**

It is lamentable that early ethnographers did not pay much attention to Indian lady's names. This lady is recorded simply as *wife of Victorianno, chief of the Soboba people.* The man is Victorianno, her husband. Both appear to be in their autumn years and life has not been overly kind to either. Although Mr. Victorianno is referred to herein as *Chief*, there never was such a position as *Chief* in Southern California. In all probability, Mr. Victorianno was a spiritual leader and non-Indians were unable, or unwilling, to distinguish between the two. The photographer is unknown.

## App.1-1
## Summary of Basket Characteristics
## Generic Luiseño Baskets

| MUSEUM ACCESSION NO. | | A1 7 | A1 39 | A1 41 | A1 50 | A1 52 | A1 54 | A1 55 | A1 56 | A1 58 | A1 59 |
|---|---|---|---|---|---|---|---|---|---|---|---|
| 1. SHAPE | TRAY | - | - | X | - | - | - | - | - | - | - |
| | BASIN/BOWL | X | X | - | X | X | X | X | X | X | X |
| | GLOBULAR | - | - | - | - | - | - | - | - | - | - |
| | OLLA/SPITTOON | - | - | - | - | - | - | - | - | - | - |
| | BURDEN /STOR. | - | - | - | - | - | - | - | - | - | - |
| | OVAL/BOAT | - | - | - | - | - | - | - | - | - | - |
| | CYLINDRICAL | - | - | - | - | - | - | - | - | - | - |
| | "OTHER" | - | - | - | - | - | - | - | - | - | - |
| 2. BOTTOM | FLAT | X | - | X | X | X | - | - | X | X | X |
| | CONCAVE | - | X | - | - | - | X | X | - | - | - |
| | CONVEX | - | - | - | - | - | - | - | - | - | - |
| 3. SIDES | VERTICAL | X | - | - | - | X | - | - | - | - | - |
| | FLARING | X | X | - | X | - | X | X | X | X | X |
| | CURVED | - | - | - | X | X | X | X | X | - | X |
| | SHOULDER | - | - | - | - | - | - | - | - | - | - |
| | BELLY | - | - | - | - | - | - | - | - | - | - |
| | "OLLA" | - | - | - | - | - | - | - | - | - | - |
| 4. TERMINAL | 0-2" | X | X | X | X | X | X | - | X | - | UNK |
| | 2+" | - | - | - | - | - | - | - | - | - | - |
| 5. BACK STITCH | 0 | - | - | X | - | X | - | - | - | - | - |
| | 1-5 | - | X | - | X | - | - | - | X | - | - |
| | 5+ | X | - | - | - | - | X | X | - | X | - |
| 6. "START" | KNOT | X | - | - | - | - | - | X | - | X | X |
| | BENT FINGER | - | X | X | - | - | X | - | X | - | - |
| | WAD | - | - | - | X | X | - | - | - | - | - |
| | FIBER | X | - | X | - | - | - | X | X | X | X |
| | JUNCUS | - | - | - | - | - | - | - | - | - | - |
| | GRASS | X | X | - | X | X | X | X | - | - | - |
| 7. FAG END | BUFES | X | X | X | X | X | X | X | X | X | X |
| | CLIPPED | - | - | - | - | - | - | - | - | - | - |
| | BOTH | - | - | - | - | - | - | - | - | - | - |
| 8. FOUND | GRASS | X | X | X | X | X | X | X | X | X | X |
| | RODS | - | - | - | - | - | - | - | - | - | - |
| | JUNCUS | - | - | - | - | - | - | - | - | - | - |
| 9. STITCH | JUNCUS | - | - | - | - | - | X | - | - | - | - |
| | SUMAC | X | X | X | X | X | - | X | X | X | X |
| | BOTH | - | - | - | - | - | - | - | - | - | - |
| 10. PATTERN | RED JUNCUS | - | - | - | X | - | - | - | - | - | - |
| | BLK JUNCUS | X | X | X | X | X | X | X | X | X | X |
| | YUCCA ROOT | - | - | - | - | - | - | X | - | - | - |
| | NEGATIVE | X | - | - | - | - | - | - | - | - | - |
| | AUSTERE | - | - | - | - | - | X | - | X | - | - |
| | MILDLY COMP. | X | X | X | X | X | - | X | - | X | X |
| | COMPLEX | - | - | - | - | - | - | - | - | - | - |
| 11. PAT. ORIEN. | VERTICAL | - | - | X | X | - | - | - | X | - | - |
| | HORIZONTAL | - | X | - | - | X | X | - | X | X | X |
| | SPIRAL | X | - | - | - | - | - | - | - | - | - |
| | STACKED | X | - | - | X | - | X | - | X | - | - |
| | CONCENTRIC | - | - | - | - | - | - | X | - | X | - |
| | STAIR STEP | X | X | - | - | - | - | - | - | - | X |
| | RANDOM | - | - | - | - | - | - | - | X | - | - |
| 12. MOTIF | GEOMETRIC | X | X | X | X | X | X | X | X | X | X |
| | ZOOMORPH. | - | - | - | - | - | - | - | - | - | - |
| | ANTHRO. | - | - | - | - | - | - | - | - | - | - |
| | NATURE | - | - | - | - | - | - | - | - | - | - |
| | FLORAL | - | - | X | - | - | - | X | - | - | - |
| | BAND | X | - | - | - | X | X | - | - | X | - |
| | BLOCK | X | - | - | - | - | - | - | - | - | - |
| 13. ANOMALY | YES | - | - | - | - | X | X | - | X | - | - |
| 14. SIGNATURE | YES | - | - | - | - | - | - | - | - | - | - |

App. 1-2
Summary of Basket Characteristics
Generic Luiseño Baskets

| MUSEUM ACCESSION NO. | | A1 60 | A1 63 | A1 65 | A1 67 | A1 68 | A1 78 | A1 79 | A1 82 | A1 86 | A1 87 |
|---|---|---|---|---|---|---|---|---|---|---|---|
| 1. SHAPE | TRAY | - | - | - | X | - | - | - | - | - | X |
| | BASIN/BOWL | X | X | X | - | - | X | - | - | X | X |
| | GLOBULAR | - | - | - | - | - | - | X | - | - | - |
| | OLLA/SPITTOON | - | - | - | - | - | - | X | - | - | - |
| | BURDEN /STOR. | - | - | - | - | X | - | - | - | X | - |
| | OVAL/BOAT | - | - | - | - | - | - | - | - | - | - |
| | CYLINDRICAL | - | - | - | - | - | - | - | - | - | - |
| | "OTHER" | - | - | - | - | - | - | - | - | - | - |
| 2. BOTTOM | FLAT | X | X | - | X | X | - | X | X | - | - |
| | CONCAVE | - | - | X | - | - | X | - | - | X | X |
| | CONVEX | - | - | - | - | - | - | - | - | - | - |
| 3. SIDES | VERTICAL | - | - | - | - | - | - | - | - | - | - |
| | FLARING | X | X | X | X | X | X | - | X | X | X |
| | CURVED | X | X | X | - | - | X | X | X | - | X |
| | SHOULDER | - | - | - | - | - | - | - | - | - | - |
| | BELLY | - | - | - | - | - | - | X | - | - | - |
| | "OLLA" | - | - | - | - | - | - | X | - | - | - |
| 4. TERMINAL | 0-2" | - | - | X | - | X | X | X | X | X | X |
| | 2+" | X | X | - | X | - | - | - | - | - | - |
| 5. BACK STITCH | 0 | - | - | - | - | - | - | - | - | X | X |
| | 1-5 | - | - | - | - | X | - | X | X | - | - |
| | 5+ | X | X | X | X | - | X | - | - | - | - |
| 6. "START" | KNOT | - | - | - | - | - | X | - | - | - | - |
| | BENT FINGER | - | - | X | - | - | - | - | - | - | X |
| | WAD | X | X | - | X | X | - | X | X | X | - |
| | FIBER | - | - | - | - | - | X | - | - | - | X |
| | JUNCUS | - | - | - | - | - | - | X | X | X | X |
| | GRASS | X | X | X | X | X | - | - | X | X | X |
| 7. FAG END | BUFES | X | X | X | X | X | X | X | X | X | X |
| | CLIPPED | - | - | - | - | - | - | - | - | - | - |
| | BOTH | - | - | - | - | - | - | - | - | - | - |
| 8. FOUND | GRASS | X | X | X | X | X | X | X | X | X | - |
| | RODS | - | - | - | - | - | - | - | - | - | - |
| | JUNCUS | - | - | - | - | - | X | X | - | - | X |
| 9. STITCH | JUNCUS | - | - | - | - | - | - | - | - | - | - |
| | SUMAC | X | X | X | X | X | X | X | X | X | X |
| | BOTH | - | - | - | - | - | - | - | - | - | - |
| 10. PATTERN | RED JUNCUS | - | - | X | X | - | - | - | - | - | - |
| | BLK JUNCUS | X | X | X | X | X | X | X | X | X | - |
| | YUCCA ROOT | - | - | - | - | - | - | - | - | - | - |
| | NEGATIVE | X | X | - | - | - | - | - | - | - | - |
| | AUSTERE | - | - | - | - | - | - | - | - | - | - |
| | MILDLY COMP. | X | X | X | X | X | - | X | - | - | - |
| | COMPLEX | - | - | - | - | - | X | - | X | - | - |
| 11. PAT. ORIEN. | VERTICAL | - | - | - | - | - | - | - | - | - | - |
| | HORIZONTAL | X | - | X | X | X | X | X | X | - | - |
| | SPIRAL | - | X | - | - | - | - | - | X | - | - |
| | STACKED | - | - | - | - | X | - | - | - | - | - |
| | CONCENTRIC | - | - | X | - | - | - | - | - | - | - |
| | STAIR STEP | - | X | X | - | X | - | - | - | - | - |
| | RANDOM | - | - | - | - | - | X | - | - | X | - |
| 12. MOTIF | GEOMETRIC | X | X | - | X | X | X | X | - | X | - |
| | ZOOMORPH. | - | - | - | - | - | - | - | - | - | - |
| | ANTHRO. | - | - | - | - | - | - | - | X | - | - |
| | NATURE | - | - | - | - | - | - | - | X | - | - |
| | FLORAL | - | - | - | - | - | - | - | - | - | - |
| | BAND | X | - | - | X | - | X | X | X | - | - |
| | BLOCK | X | X | - | - | - | - | - | - | - | - |
| 13. ANOMALY | YES | X | - | - | - | - | X | - | - | - | - |
| 14. SIGNATURE | YES | - | - | - | - | - | - | - | - | - | - |

## Summary of Basket Characteristics
### Generic Luiseño Baskets

| MUSEUM ACCESSION NO. | | A1 88 | A1 89 | A1 92 | A1 94 | A1 95 | A1 96 | A1 97 | A1 99 | A1 138 | A8 120 |
|---|---|---|---|---|---|---|---|---|---|---|---|
| 1. SHAPE | TRAY | - | - | - | - | - | - | - | X | - | - |
| | BASIN/BOWL | X | X | - | - | - | X | X | - | X | X |
| | GLOBULAR | - | - | - | - | - | - | - | - | - | - |
| | OLLA/SPITTOON | - | - | - | - | - | - | - | - | - | - |
| | BURDEN /STOR. | - | - | X | X | X | - | - | - | - | - |
| | OVAL/BOAT | - | - | - | - | - | - | - | - | - | - |
| | CYLINDRICAL | - | - | - | - | - | - | - | - | - | - |
| | "OTHER" | - | - | - | - | - | - | - | - | - | - |
| 2. BOTTOM | FLAT | - | X | - | X | X | X | - | - | X | - |
| | CONCAVE | - | - | X | - | - | - | X | X | - | X |
| | CONVEX | X | - | - | - | - | - | - | - | - | - |
| 3. SIDES | VERTICAL | - | - | - | - | - | - | - | - | - | - |
| | FLARING | - | X | X | X | X | X | X | X | X | X |
| | CURVED | - | X | X | - | - | X | X | - | X | X |
| | SHOULDER | - | - | - | - | - | - | - | - | - | - |
| | BELLY | - | - | - | - | - | - | - | - | - | - |
| | "OLLA" | - | - | - | - | - | - | - | - | - | - |
| 4. TERMINAL | 0-2" | - | UNk | X | - | - | UNK | - | X | X | X |
| | 2+" | - | - | - | X | X | - | X | - | - | - |
| 5. BACK STITCH | 0 | - | UNK | - | - | - | UNK | - | - | - | X |
| | 1-5 | - | - | X | - | - | - | X | X | X | - |
| | 5+ | - | - | - | X | - | - | - | - | - | - |
| 6. "START" | KNOT | - | - | - | - | X | - | - | - | - | X |
| | BENT FINGER | - | - | X | - | - | - | X | - | X | - |
| | WAD | - | X | - | X | - | X | - | - | - | - |
| | FIBER | - | X | - | - | X | - | - | - | - | - |
| | JUNCUS | - | - | - | - | - | - | - | - | - | X |
| | GRASS | - | - | X | X | - | X | X | - | X | - |
| 7. FAG END | BUFES | - | X | X | X | X | X | X | X | X | X |
| | CLIPPED | - | - | - | - | - | - | - | - | - | - |
| | BOTH | - | - | - | - | - | - | - | - | - | - |
| 8. FOUND | GRASS | - | X | X | X | X | X | X | X | X | X |
| | RODS | - | - | - | - | - | - | - | - | - | - |
| | JUNCUS | - | - | - | - | - | - | - | - | X | - |
| 9. STITCH | JUNCUS | - | - | - | X | X | - | - | - | - | - |
| | SUMAC | - | X | X | - | - | X | X | X | X | X |
| | BOTH | - | - | - | - | - | - | - | - | - | - |
| 10. PATTERN | RED JUNCUS | - | - | X | - | - | - | - | - | - | X |
| | BLK JUNCUS | - | X | X | X | X | X | X | X | X | X |
| | YUCCA ROOT | - | - | - | - | - | - | - | - | - | - |
| | NEGATIVE | - | - | - | - | - | - | - | - | - | - |
| | AUSTERE | - | X | - | X | X | X | - | - | - | - |
| | MILDLY COMP. | - | - | X | - | - | - | X | X | X | X |
| | COMPLEX | - | - | - | - | - | - | - | - | - | - |
| 11. PAT. ORIEN. | VERTICAL | - | - | - | - | - | - | - | - | - | X |
| | HORIZONTAL | - | X | X | X | X | X | X | X | - | - |
| | SPIRAL | - | - | - | - | - | - | X | - | X | - |
| | STACKED | - | - | - | - | - | - | - | - | - | X |
| | CONCENTRIC | - | - | X | - | - | X | - | - | - | - |
| | STAIR STEP | - | - | - | - | - | - | X | - | X | - |
| | RANDOM | - | - | - | - | - | - | - | X | - | - |
| 12. MOTIF | GEOMETRIC | - | X | X | X | - | X | X | X | X | X |
| | ZOOMORPH. | - | - | - | - | - | - | - | - | - | - |
| | ANTHRO. | - | - | - | - | - | - | - | - | - | - |
| | NATURE | - | - | - | - | - | - | - | - | - | - |
| | FLORAL | - | - | - | - | - | - | - | - | - | - |
| | BAND | - | - | X | X | X | - | - | - | X | - |
| | BLOCK | - | - | - | - | - | - | - | X | - | - |
| 13. ANOMALY | YES | - | - | - | X | - | - | - | - | - | - |
| 14. SIGNATURE | YES | - | - | - | - | - | - | - | - | | |

# App. 1-4
## Summary of Basket Characteristics
## Generic Luiseño Baskets

| MUSEUM ACCESSION NO. | | A8 129 | A11 2 | A31 5 | A83 262 | A83 263 | A83 277 | A83 297 | A116 1 | A144 8 | A144 11 |
|---|---|---|---|---|---|---|---|---|---|---|---|
| 1. SHAPE | TRAY | - | - | - | X- | X | X | - | - | - | - |
| | BASIN/BOWL | X | - | - | - | - | - | - | - | X | - |
| | GLOBULAR | - | - | - | - | - | - | - | - | - | - |
| | OLLA/SPITTOON | - | - | - | - | - | - | - | - | - | - |
| | BURDEN /STOR. | - | X | X | - | - | - | X | X | - | X |
| | OVAL/BOAT | - | - | - | - | - | - | - | - | - | - |
| | CYLINDRICAL | - | - | - | - | - | - | - | - | - | - |
| | "OTHER" | - | - | - | - | - | - | - | - | - | - |
| 2. BOTTOM | FLAT | X | X | X | - | X | X | X | X | X | X |
| | CONCAVE | - | - | - | X | - | - | - | - | - | - |
| | CONVEX | - | - | - | - | - | - | - | - | - | - |
| 3. SIDES | VERTICAL | - | - | X | - | - | - | - | - | - | - |
| | FLARING | - | X | - | X | X | X | X | X | X | X |
| | CURVED | X | - | X | - | - | X | - | - | - | - |
| | SHOULDER | - | - | - | - | - | - | - | - | - | - |
| | BELLY | X | - | - | - | - | - | - | - | - | - |
| | "OLLA" | - | - | - | - | - | - | - | - | - | - |
| 4. TERMINAL | 0-2" | X | UNK | - | X | X | X | UNK | X | X | - |
| | 2+" | - | - | X | - | - | - | - | - | - | X |
| 5. BACK STITCH | 0 | - | UNK | - | X | X | - | UNK | - | - | - |
| | 1-5 | X | - | X | - | - | X | - | X | X | X |
| | 5+ | - | - | - | - | - | - | - | - | - | - |
| 6. "START" | KNOT | - | X | - | - | - | - | - | - | - | - |
| | BENT FINGER | - | - | X | - | - | X | - | - | - | X |
| | WAD | X | - | - | - | X | - | X | X | X | - |
| | FIBER | - | X | - | - | - | - | - | - | - | - |
| | JUNCUS | - | - | - | - | - | - | - | - | - | - |
| | GRASS | X | X | X | - | X | X | X | X | X | X |
| 7. FAG END | BUFES | X | - | X | - | X | X | X | X | X | X |
| | CLIPPED | - | - | - | X | - | - | - | - | - | - |
| | BOTH | - | - | - | - | - | - | - | - | - | - |
| 8. FOUND | GRASS | X | X | X | X | X | X | X | X | X | X |
| | RODS | - | - | - | - | - | - | - | - | - | - |
| | JUNCUS | - | - | - | - | - | - | - | - | - | - |
| 9. STITCH | JUNCUS | - | X | - | X | - | - | - | - | - | - |
| | SUMAC | X | - | X | - | X | - | X | X | X | X |
| | BOTH | - | - | - | - | - | X | - | - | - | - |
| 10. PATTERN | RED JUNCUS | X | - | - | - | X | X | - | - | - | - |
| | BLK JUNCUS | X | X | X | X | X | X | X | X | X | X |
| | YUCCA ROOT | - | - | - | - | - | - | - | - | - | - |
| | NEGATIVE | - | - | - | - | - | - | - | - | - | - |
| | AUSTERE | - | - | X | X | - | X | X | - | X | - |
| | MILDLY COMP. | X | X | - | - | X | - | - | X | - | X |
| | COMPLEX | - | - | - | - | - | - | - | - | - | - |
| 11. PAT. ORIEN. | VERTICAL | - | X | - | - | - | - | - | - | X | - |
| | HORIZONTAL | X | - | X | X | X | X | X | X | - | X |
| | SPIRAL | - | - | - | - | - | - | - | - | - | - |
| | STACKED | - | - | - | - | - | - | - | - | X | - |
| | CONCENTRIC | - | - | - | - | - | - | - | X | - | - |
| | STAIR STEP | - | - | - | X | - | X | - | - | - | - |
| | RANDOM | - | - | - | X | - | - | - | - | - | - |
| 12. MOTIF | GEOMETRIC | - | - | X | X | X | X | X | X | X | X |
| | ZOOMORPH. | - | - | - | - | - | - | - | - | - | - |
| | ANTHRO. | - | - | - | - | - | - | - | - | - | - |
| | NATURE | X | X | - | - | - | - | - | - | - | - |
| | FLORAL | - | - | - | - | - | - | - | - | - | - |
| | BAND | X | X | - | X | X | - | X | X | - | X |
| | BLOCK | - | - | - | X | - | - | - | - | - | - |
| 13. ANOMALY | YES | - | - | - | - | - | - | - | - | - | - |
| 14. SIGNATURE | YES | - | X | X | - | - | - | - | - | - | - |

## Summary of Basket Characteristics
### Generic Luiseño Baskets

| MUSEUM ACCESSION NO. | | A313 13 | A319 1(2) | A319 1 (3) | A955 2 | A1236 11 | A1236 18 | A1236 36 | A1236 37 | A1236 39 | A1236 40 |
|---|---|---|---|---|---|---|---|---|---|---|---|
| 1. SHAPE | TRAY | - | X | X | - | - | - | - | - | - | - |
| | BASIN/BOWL | X | - | - | - | X | X | - | - | - | - |
| | GLOBULAR | - | - | - | - | - | - | - | - | - | - |
| | OLLA/SPITTOON | - | - | - | - | - | - | - | - | - | - |
| | BURDEN /STOR. | - | - | - | X | - | - | X | X | X | X |
| | OVAL/BOAT | - | - | - | - | - | - | - | - | - | - |
| | CYLINDRICAL | - | - | - | - | - | - | - | - | - | - |
| | "OTHER" | - | - | - | - | - | - | - | - | - | - |
| 2. BOTTOM | FLAT | - | - | X | - | X | X | X | X | X | X |
| | CONCAVE | - | X | - | X | - | - | - | - | - | - |
| | CONVEX | X | - | - | - | - | - | - | - | - | - |
| 3. SIDES | VERTICAL | - | - | - | - | - | - | - | - | - | - |
| | FLARING | X | X | X | X | - | - | X | X | X | X |
| | CURVED | X | X | - | - | X | X | X | - | X | X |
| | SHOULDER | - | - | - | - | - | - | - | - | - | - |
| | BELLY | - | - | - | - | X | X | - | - | - | - |
| | "OLLA" | - | - | - | - | - | - | - | - | - | - |
| 4. TERMINAL | 0-2" | X | - | UNK | - | X | - | X | - | X | UNK |
| | 2+" | - | X | - | X | - | X | - | X | - | - |
| 5. BACK STITCH | 0 | - | - | UNK | - | - | - | - | - | - | UNK |
| | 1-5 | X | X- | - | X | - | X | X | - | X | - |
| | 5+ | - | - | - | - | X | - | - | X | - | - |
| 6. "START" | KNOT | X | - | - | - | - | - | - | X | - | - |
| | BENT FINGER | - | X | - | - | X | X | X | - | X | - |
| | WAD | - | - | X | X | - | - | - | - | - | X |
| | FIBER | - | - | - | - | - | X | - | X | X | - |
| | JUNCUS | - | X | - | - | - | - | - | - | - | - |
| | GRASS | X | X | X | X | X | X | X | - | - | X |
| 7. FAG END | BUFES | X | - | X | X | X | X | X | X | X | X |
| | CLIPPED | - | - | - | - | - | - | - | - | - | - |
| | BOTH | - | X | - | - | - | - | - | - | - | - |
| 8. FOUND | GRASS | X | X | X | X | X | X | X | X | X | X |
| | RODS | - | - | - | - | - | - | - | - | - | - |
| | JUNCUS | - | - | - | - | - | - | - | - | - | - |
| 9. STITCH | JUNCUS | - | X | X | - | - | - | - | - | X | - |
| | SUMAC | X | - | - | X | X | - | X | X | - | X |
| | BOTH | - | X | - | X | - | X | - | - | - | - |
| 10. PATTERN | RED JUNCUS | - | - | - | - | - | - | - | X | - | - |
| | BLK JUNCUS | X | X | X | X | X | X | X | X | X | X |
| | YUCCA ROOT | - | - | - | - | - | - | - | - | - | - |
| | NEGATIVE | - | - | - | - | - | - | - | - | - | - |
| | AUSTERE | - | - | X | - | - | - | - | - | X | - |
| | MILDLY COMP. | X | - | - | X | X | - | X | X | - | X |
| | COMPLEX | - | X | - | - | - | X | - | - | - | - |
| 11. PAT. ORIEN. | VERTICAL | - | - | - | - | - | - | - | - | X | - |
| | HORIZONTAL | - | - | X | X | - | - | X | X | - | - |
| | SPIRAL | X | X | - | - | - | - | - | - | - | - |
| | STACKED | - | X | - | - | - | - | X | - | X | - |
| | CONCENTRIC | - | - | - | - | - | - | - | X | - | - |
| | STAIR STEP | X | X | - | - | - | - | - | - | - | x |
| | RANDOM | - | - | - | - | X | X | - | - | - | - |
| 12. MOTIF | GEOMETRIC | X | X | - | X | - | - | X | X | X | X |
| | ZOOMORPH. | - | - | - | - | - | - | - | - | - | - |
| | ANTHRO. | - | - | - | - | - | - | - | - | - | - |
| | NATURE | - | - | - | - | - | - | - | - | - | - |
| | FLORAL | - | - | - | - | X | X | - | - | X | - |
| | BAND | - | X | X | X | - | - | X | X | X | - |
| | BLOCK | X | X | - | - | X | - | - | - | - | - |
| 13. ANOMALY | YES | - | - | - | - | - | - | - | - | - | - |
| 14. SIGNATURE | YES | - | - | - | - | - | - | - | - | - | - |

# Summary of Basket Characteristics
## Generic Luiseño Baskets

| MUSEUM ACCESSION NO. | | A1236 45 | A1236 47 | A1240 3 | A1236 6 | A1240 7 | A1240 9 |
|---|---|---|---|---|---|---|---|
| 1. SHAPE | TRAY | - | - | - | - | - | - |
| | BASIN/BOWL | X | X | X | - | - | - |
| | GLOBULAR | - | - | - | X | - | X |
| | OLLA/SPITTOON | - | - | - | - | - | - |
| | BURDEN /STOR. | - | - | - | - | X | - |
| | OVAL/BOAT | - | - | - | - | - | - |
| | CYLINDRICAL | - | - | - | - | - | - |
| | "OTHER" | - | - | - | - | - | - |
| 2. BOTTOM | FLAT | X | X | X | - | X | X |
| | CONCAVE | - | X | - | X | - | - |
| | CONVEX | - | - | - | X | - | - |
| 3. SIDES | VERTICAL | - | - | - | - | - | - |
| | FLARING | X | X | X | X | X | - |
| | CURVED | - | X | - | - | - | X |
| | SHOULDER | - | - | - | - | - | X |
| | BELLY | - | - | - | - | - | - |
| | "OLLA" | - | - | - | - | - | - |
| 4. TERMINAL | 0-2" | - | - | X | X | UNK | UNK |
| | 2+" | X | X | - | - | - | - |
| 5. BACK STITCH | 0 | - | | - | - | UNK | UNK |
| | 1-5 | X | - | X | - | - | - |
| | 5+ | - | X | - | X | - | - |
| 6. "START" | KNOT | - | - | - | - | - | UNK |
| | BENT FINGER | X | X | X | X | - | - |
| | WAD | - | - | - | - | X | - |
| | FIBER | - | - | - | - | X | - |
| | JUNCUS | - | | - | - | - | - |
| | GRASS | X | X | X | X | - | - |
| 7. FAG END | BUFES | X | X | X | X | X | X |
| | CLIPPED | - | - | - | - | - | - |
| | BOTH | - | - | - | - | - | - |
| 8. FOUND | GRASS | X | X | X | X | X | - |
| | RODS | - | - | - | - | - | - |
| | JUNCUS | - | - | - | - | - | X |
| 9. STITCH | JUNCUS | - | X | - | - | - | - |
| | SUMAC | X | - | X | X | X | X |
| | BOTH | - | - | - | - | - | - |
| 10. PATTERN | RED JUNCUS | - | X | - | X | - | - |
| | BLK JUNCUS | - | X | X | X | X | X |
| | YUCCA ROOT | - | - | - | - | - | - |
| | NEGATIVE | - | - | - | - | - | X |
| | AUSTERE | - | - | - | - | - | - |
| | MILDLY COMP. | X | X | - | X | X | X |
| | COMPLEX | - | - | X | - | - | - |
| 11. PAT. ORIEN. | VERTICAL X | - | - | X | - | - | |
| | HORIZONTAL | X | X | X | - | X | X |
| | SPIRAL | - | - | - | - | - | - |
| | STACKED | X | - | - | X | - | - |
| | CONCENTRIC | - | X | - | - | X | X |
| | STAIR STEP | - | - | - | - | - | - |
| | RANDOM | - | - | X | - | - | - |
| 12. MOTIF | GEOMETRIC | X | X | - | X | X | X |
| | ZOOMORPH. | - | - | X | - | - | - |
| | ANTHRO. | - | - | X | - | - | - |
| | NATURE | - | - | - | - | - | - |
| | FLORAL | - | X | - | X | - | - |
| | BAND | X | - | X | X | - | - |
| | BLOCK | - | - | - | - | - | - |
| 13. ANOMALY | YES | - | - | - | - | - | - |
| 14. SIGNATURE | YES | X | X | - | X | - | - |

# App. 2-1
## Summary of Basket Characteristics
## Generic Soboba Baskets

| MUSEUM ACCESSION NO. | | A1 29 | A1 53 | A1 71 | A1 80 | A8 3 | A83 291 | A83 292 | A1236 34 |
|---|---|---|---|---|---|---|---|---|---|
| 1. SHAPE | TRAY | - | - | - | - | - | - | X | X |
| | BASIN/BOWL | - | X | - | - | X | - | - | - |
| | GLOBULAR | - | - | X | X | - | - | - | - |
| | OLLA/SPITTOON | - | - | - | ⌐ | - | X | - | - |
| | BURDEN /STOR. | - | - | - | - | - | - | - | - |
| | OVAL/BOAT | X | - | - | - | - | - | - | - |
| | CYLINDRICAL | - | - | - | - | - | - | - | - |
| | "OTHER" | - | - | - | - | - | - | - | - |
| 2. BOTTOM | FLAT | X | X | - | X | X | X | X | X |
| | CONCAVE | - | - | - | - | - | - | - | - |
| | CONVEX | - | - | X | - | - | - | - | - |
| 3. SIDES | VERTICAL | - | - | - | - | - | - | - | - |
| | FLARING | - | X | X | - | - | - | X | X |
| | CURVED | X | X | - | X | X | X | - | - |
| | SHOULDER | - | - | - | - | - | - | - | - |
| | BELLY | - | - | X | X | - | X | - | - |
| | "OLLA" | - | - | - | - | - | - | - | - |
| 4. TERMINAL | 0-2" | X | X | UNK | X | - | - | X | X |
| | 2+" | - | - | - | - | X | X | - | - |
| 5. BACK STITCH | 0 | - | X | UNK | X | X | - | - | - |
| | 1-5 | X | - | - | - | - | - | X | X |
| | 5+ | - | - | - | - | - | X | - | - |
| 6. "START" | KNOT | - | - | - | - | - | - | - | X |
| | BENT FINGER | X | X | X | X | - | - | - | - |
| | WAD | - | - | - | - | X | X | X | - |
| | FIBER | - | X | - | - | - | - | - | - |
| | JUNCUS | - | - | - | - | - | - | - | - |
| | GRASS | X | - | X | X | X | X | X | X |
| 7. FAG END | BUFES | X | X | X | X | X | X | X | X |
| | CLIPPED | - | - | - | - | - | - | - | - |
| | BOTH | - | - | - | - | - | - | - | - |
| 8. FOUND | GRASS | X | X | X | X | X | X | X | X |
| | RODS | - | - | - | - | - | - | - | - |
| | JUNCUS | - | - | - | - | - | - | - | - |
| 9. STITCH | JUNCUS | - | - | - | - | - | - | - | - |
| | SUMAC | - | X | X | X | X | - | - | X |
| | BOTH | X | - | - | - | - | X | X | - |
| 10. PATTERN | RED JUNCUS | X | - | - | - | - | - | - | X |
| | BLK JUNCUS | X | X | X | X | X | X | X | X |
| | YUCCA ROOT | - | - | - | - | - | - | - | - |
| | NEGATIVE | - | - | - | - | - | - | - | - |
| | AUSTERE | - | - | - | - | - | X | X | - |
| | MILDLY COMP. | - | X | - | X | - | - | - | X |
| | COMPLEX | X | - | X | - | X | - | - | - |
| 11. PAT. ORIEN. | VERTICAL | X | - | - | - | - | - | - | - |
| | HORIZONTAL | - | X | - | X | - | X | X | - |
| | SPIRAL | - | - | - | - | - | - | - | X |
| | STACKED | X | - | X | - | - | - | - | - |
| | CONCENTRIC | - | - | - | - | - | - | - | - |
| | STAIR STEP | - | - | - | - | - | X | - | X |
| | RANDOM | - | - | - | - | X | - | - | - |
| 12. MOTIF | GEOMETRIC | - | X | X | X | X | X | - | X |
| | ZOOMORPH. | - | - | - | - | - | - | - | - |
| | ANTHRO. | - | - | - | - | - | - | - | - |
| | NATURE | - | - | - | - | - | - | - | - |
| | FLORAL | X | - | - | - | - | - | - | - |
| | BAND | X | - | - | - | - | X | X | X |
| | BLOCK | - | - | - | - | - | - | - | - |
| 13. ANOMALY | YES | - | - | - | - | - | - | - | - |
| 14. SIGNATURE | YES | - | - | - | - | - | - | - | - |

## Summary of Basket Characteristics
## Pechanga, Pala, Rincon, and La Jolla Baskets

| MUSEUM ACCESSION NO. | | A8 95 | A8 96 | A8 97 | A8 98 | A8 99 | A8 100 | A8 104 | A8 110 | A8 118 |
|---|---|---|---|---|---|---|---|---|---|---|
| 1. SHAPE | TRAY | - | - | - | - | - | - | - | - | - |
| | BASIN/BOWL | X | X | X | X | X | X | X | X | X |
| | GLOBULAR | - | - | - | - | - | - | - | - | - |
| | OLLA/SPITTOON | - | - | - | - | - | - | - | X | - |
| | BURDEN /STOR. | - | - | - | - | - | - | - | - | - |
| | OVAL/BOAT | - | - | - | - | - | - | - | - | - |
| | CYLINDRICAL | - | - | - | - | - | - | - | - | - |
| | "OTHER" | - | - | - | - | - | - | - | - | - |
| 2. BOTTOM | FLAT | X | - | X | X | X | X | X | X | X |
| | CONCAVE | - | X | - | X | - | - | - | - | - |
| | CONVEX | - | - | - | - | - | - | - | - | - |
| 3. SIDES | VERTICAL | - | - | - | - | - | - | - | - | - |
| | FLARING | X | X | X | X | X | X | X | X | X |
| | CURVED | X | - | - | X | X | - | - | - | - |
| | SHOULDER | - | - | - | - | - | - | - | - | - |
| | BELLY | - | - | - | - | - | - | - | - | - |
| | "OLLA" | - | - | - | - | - | - | - | - | - |
| 4. TERMINAL | 0-2" | X | X | X | X | - | X | X | X | - |
| | 2+" | - | - | - | - | X | - | - | - | X |
| 5. BACK STITCH | 0 | X | - | X | - | X | X | X | X | X |
| | 1-5 | - | X | - | X | - | - | - | - | - |
| | 5+ | - | - | - | - | - | - | - | - | - |
| 6. "START" | KNOT | X | - | - | - | - | - | - | X | - |
| | BENT FINGER | - | X | X | X | X | X | X | - | X |
| | WAD | - | - | - | - | - | - | - | - | - |
| | FIBER | X | - | - | - | - | X | - | - | - |
| | JUNCUS | - | - | - | - | - | - | - | - | - |
| | GRASS | - | X | X | X | X | - | X | X | X |
| 7. FAG END | BUFES | X | X | X | X | X | X | X | X | - |
| | CLIPPED | - | - | - | - | - | - | - | - | - |
| | BOTH | - | - | - | - | - | - | - | - | X |
| 8. FOUND | GRASS | X | X | X | X | X | X | X | X | X |
| | RODS | - | - | - | - | - | - | - | - | - |
| | JUNCUS | - | - | - | - | - | - | - | - | - |
| 9. STITCH | JUNCUS | X | - | X | - | X | - | - | - | X |
| | SUMAC | - | - | - | X | - | - | X | - | - |
| | BOTH | - | X | - | - | - | X | - | X | - |
| 10. PATTERN | RED JUNCUS | X | X | - | X | X | X | X | X | X |
| | BLK JUNCUS | X | X | X | X | X | X | X | X | X |
| | YUCCA ROOT | - | - | - | - | - | - | - | - | - |
| | NEGATIVE | - | - | X | - | X | - | - | - | - |
| | AUSTERE | - | - | - | - | - | - | - | - | - |
| | MILDLY COMP. | - | - | - | - | X | - | - | - | X |
| | COMPLEX | X | X | X | X | - | X | X | X | - |
| 11. PAT. ORIEN. | VERTICAL | - | X | - | X | - | X | - | X | - |
| | HORIZONTAL | - | X | - | - | - | X | - | - | X |
| | SPIRAL | - | - | - | - | X | - | X | - | - |
| | STACKED | X | - | - | X | X | - | - | - | - |
| | CONCENTRIC | X | - | - | - | - | - | - | - | X |
| | STAIR STEP | - | - | - | - | - | - | X | - | - |
| | RANDOM | X | - | X | X | - | X | X | - | - |
| 12. MOTIF | GEOMETRIC | X | X | X | X | X | X | - | - | X |
| | ZOOMORPH. | - | - | - | X | - | X | X | - | - |
| | ANTHRO. | - | - | - | - | - | - | X | - | - |
| | NATURE | - | - | - | X | X | - | - | - | - |
| | FLORAL | X | - | X | - | - | - | - | X | - |
| | BAND | - | - | X | X | - | - | X | - | - |
| | BLOCK | - | - | - | - | - | - | - | - | - |
| 13. ANOMALY | YES | - | X | - | X | - | - | X | - | - |
| 14. SIGNATURE | YES | - | X | - | - | - | - | - | - | - |

Summary of Basket Characteristics
Pechanga, Pala, Rincon, And La Jolla Baskets

| MUSEUM ACCESSION NO. | | A8 122 | A8 124 | A8 128 |
|---|---|---|---|---|
| **1. SHAPE** | TRAY | - | - | - |
| | BASIN/BOWL | X | X | X |
| | GLOBULAR | - | - | - |
| | OLLA/SPITTOON | - | - | - |
| | BURDEN /STOR. | - | - | - |
| | OVAL/BOAT | - | - | - |
| | CYLINDRICAL | - | - | - |
| | "OTHER" | - | - | - |
| **2. BOTTOM** | FLAT | X | - | X |
| | CONCAVE | - | - | - |
| | CONVEX | - | X | - |
| **3. SIDES** | VERTICAL | - | - | - |
| | FLARING | X | - | - |
| | CURVED | - | X | X |
| | SHOULDER | - | - | - |
| | BELLY | - | - | - |
| | "OLLA" | - | - | - |
| **4. TERMINAL** | 0-2" | X | X | X |
| | 2+" | - | - | - |
| **5. BACK STITCH** | 0 | - | - | X |
| | 1-5 | X | X | - |
| | 5+ | - | - | - |
| **6. "START"** | KNOT | - | X | - |
| | BENT FINGER | X | - | X |
| | WAD | - | - | - |
| | FIBER | - | - | - |
| | JUNCUS | - | - | - |
| | GRASS | X | X | X |
| **7. FAG END** | BUFES | X | X | - |
| | CLIPPED | - | - | - |
| | BOTH | - | - | X |
| **8. FOUND** | GRASS | X | X | - |
| | RODS | - | - | - |
| | JUNCUS | - | - | - |
| **9. STITCH** | JUNCUS | - | - | - |
| | SUMAC | - | - | X |
| | BOTH | X | X | - |
| **10. PATTERN** | RED JUNCUS | X | X | X |
| | BLK JUNCUS | X | X | X |
| | YUCCA ROOT | - | - | - |
| | NEGATIVE | - | - | - |
| | AUSTERE | - | X | - |
| | MILDLY COMP. | - | - | X |
| | COMPLEX | X | - | - |
| **11. PAT. ORIEN.** | VERTICAL | - | - | - |
| | HORIZONTAL | X | X | - |
| | SPIRAL | - | - | X |
| | STACKED | - | - | - |
| | CONCENTRIC | X | - | - |
| | STAIR STEP | - | - | - |
| | RANDOM | - | - | - |
| **12. MOTIF** | GEOMETRIC | X | X | - |
| | ZOOMORPH. | - | - | - |
| | ANTHRO. | - | - | - |
| | NATURE | - | - | - |
| | FLORAL | - | - | - |
| | BAND | - | X | X |
| | BLOCK | - | - | - |
| **13. ANOMALY** | YES | - | - | - |
| **14. SIGNATURE** | YES | - | - | - |

***Mrs. Antonia Cassarera using a burden carrying net***

This photo illustrates the use of a burden carrying net by Mrs. Antonia
Cassarera, a Southern California Indian lady, circa 1920. The burden, in this
case a clay olla, is carried on the lady's back in a fiber net supported by a
*Tump Line* over her forehead. Note that Mrs. Cassarera is wearing a basketry
hat for head protection. This photo was taken by the late Edward Davis and is
from the author's collection.

# *Bibliography*

Abel-Vidor, Suzanne, Dot Brovarney, and Susan Billy
1996 *Remember Your relations, the Elsie Allen Baskets, Family and Friends.*
Berkeley, Calif.: Heyday Books

Bean, Lowell John 1978 "Cahuilla" In *Handbook of North American Indians,*
*Volume 8, California.* Edited by Robert Heizer, 575-587. Washington, D.C.,
Smithsonian Institution.

Bean, Lowell John and Florence C. Shipek
1978 "Luiseño" In *Handbook of North American Indians, Volume 8, California.*
Edited by Robert Heizer, 550–574. Washington, D.C., Smithsonian Institution.

Bean, Lowell John and Charles R. Smith
1978 "Cupeño" In *Handbook of North American Indian, Volume 8, California.*
Edited by Robert Heizer, 588–591. Washington D.C., Smithsonian Institution.

Bernstein, Bruce
2003 *The Language of Native American Baskets.* Washington and New York:
The National Museum of the American Indian.

Bibby, Brian
1996 *The Fine Art of California Indian Basketry.* Sacramento, Calif.: Crocker
Art Museum.

Busby, Sharon
2003 *Spruce Root Basketry of the Haida and Tlingit.* Seattle, Washington:
University of Washington Press.

Cain, William, basketry expert
1980–2003 personal communication.

Cain, William and Art Silva
1976 *California Indian Basketry.* Cypress, Calif.: Cypress College.

Campbell, Paul
2001 *Survival Skills of Native California.* Layton, Utah: Gibbs Smith publisher.

Dakin, Susanna Bryant
1978 *A Scotch Paisano in Los Angeles.* Los Angeles, Calif.: University of
California Press [Reprint of 1939 original].

Dalrymple, Larry
2000 *Indian Basket Makers of California and the Great Basin.* Santa Fe, NM:
University of New Mexico Press.

Davidson, Anstruther, M.D. and George Moxley
1923 *Flora of California,* Los Angels, Calif.: Times-Mirror.

Farmer, Justin F.
1993 *California Indian Baskets, Their Characteristics and Materials Used.*
Private Publication.

Farmer, Justin F. *(cont.)*

1994, *California Indian Arts Association, a  video on basketry.*

1998 *California Indian Arts Association, a video on basketry.*

1999 *California Indian Arts Association,* a video on basketry.

1999 *California Indian Arts Association, a video on pattern anomalies.*

2003 *Weaving a "Mission Basket".* Unpublished manuscript.

Farmer, Justin F. and Christopher Moser
1996 *California Indian Arts Association,* A video on "Rattlesnake" Baskets.

Farmer, Justin F. and Jan Timbrook
1998 *California Indian Arts Association, a video on basketry.*

Garbarino, Merwyn S.
1976 *Native American Heritage.* New York: Little, Brown and Co.

Hedges, Ken
1997 *Fibers and Forms: Native American Basketry of the West.* San Diego, Calif.: San Diego Museum of Man.

Heizer, Robert F. and M.A. Whipple
1951 *California Indians.* Berkeley, Calif.: University of California Press.

Heizer, Robert F. and Alan Almquist
1971 *The Other Californians.* Berkeley, Calif.: University of California Press.

Jepson, Willlis Linn
1925 *A Manual of the Flowering Plants of California.* San Francisco, Calif.: California School Book Depository.

Johnson, John, Curator, Santa Barbara Museum of Natural History
2004 Personal communication.

Kasparek, Jerry, Basket expert
1975–1985 Personal communication.

Kitchens, Joan, native plant specialist
2003 Personal communication.

Lopez, Raul A. And Christopher Moser
1981 *Rods, Bundles, and Stitches.* Riverside, Calif.: Riverside Museum Press.

Luomala, Katharine
1978 *"Tipai -Ipai".* In *Handbook of American Indian, Volume 8, California.* Edited by Robert Heizer, 592–609. Washington D.C. : Smithsonian Institution.

Mast, Edward J. F.,  rancher-cattleman
1999 Personal communication.

Moreno, Joe, Tribal Elder
1994–2004 Personal communication.

Moser, Christopher
1993 *Native American Basketry of Southern California.* Riverside, Calif.: Riverside Museum Press.

Murrell, Ruth Earl
1980 *Plants Used in Basketry by the California Indians.* Ramona, Calif.: Acoma Press [reprint].

Parker, Julia, [Kashaya Pomo], basket maker
1980–2003 Personal communication.

Parker, Lucy, [Pomo-Paiute], basket maker
    1980–2000 Personal communication.

Quinn, Charles Russell
    1962 *Mesa Grande Country.* Downey, Calif.: Elena Quinn.

Silva, Art, basket expert
    1975–1985 Personal communication.

Slater, Eva, basket expert
    1975–1985 Personal communication.

Smith, Sarah Bixby
    1974 *Adobe Days.* Fresno, Calif.: Valley Publishers [reprint of 1925 original].

Timbrook, Jan, curator
    2004 Personal communication.

Turnbaugh, Sarah Peabody, and William A. Turnbaugh
    1986 *Indian Baskets.* Westchester, Pennsylvania : Schiffer Publishing Ltd.